Susy.

Since you're
embarking
on the
dating·go·round
again.

Anng
xo

TALES
FROM THE
FRONT

TALES
FROM THE
FRONT

♥   ♥   ♥

Laura Kavesh
and Cheryl Lavin

DOLPHIN
Doubleday
NEW YORK
1988

To our families,
with love and gratitude.

Library of Congress Cataloging in Publication Data
Kavesh, Laura.
    Tales from the front: real people report from the singles scene/
Laura Kavesh and Cheryl Lavin.
        p.   cm.
    Derived from the authors' nationally syndicated column of the same
name that began in Mar. 1985: re-written and amplified with much new
material.
    ISBN 0-385-24159-3
    1. Single people—United States—Case studies.   I. Lavin, Cheryl.
II. Title.
HQ800.4.U6K38   1988
305′.0652—dc19   87–19854
                                                                              CIP

Acknowledgments

We would like to thank everyone who helped us turn an idea for a column about relationships into a reality: our friends, whose romantic adventures became our earliest material and whose encouragement has meant the world to us; the editor of the Chicago *Tribune,* Jim Squires, whose support of *Tales from the Front* has been unfailing; the Chicago *Tribune,* where portions of this material have appeared; our agent, Aaron Priest, who guided this project from its beginnings; our editor, Jennifer Brehl, who never lost her patience and good humor; and most of all, our readers, who have so generously shared their lives with us. We could never have written this book without them.

Contents

Introduction

We're friends. We met in 1983 when Laura first came to work at the Chicago *Tribune* as a feature writer. Cheryl had been on the staff since 1981. The friendship was easy. We were both single. We both like to see movies and plays and try new restaurants. So about once a week we'd get together.

And what did you know!

We didn't spend a lot of time discussing air pollution. We didn't fret over fiscal responsibility. In fact, we never even mentioned the federal deficit. We talked about relationships.

Our relationships. Our friends' relationships. The ebb and flow of them. The highs and lows of them. The beginnings, middles, and ends of them.

Now, we're not dumb. Far from it. We consider ourselves bright women with fascinating careers. As newspaper reporters we've covered everyone from Henry Kissinger to Joan Collins, Michael Jackson to Sally Field, Ollie North to Oprah Winfrey.

But when we got together, we didn't swap stories about Henry and Joan and Michael and Sally and Ollie and Oprah. We talked about our friend Jay who walked into his living room one night to find his girlfriend kissing his roommate. And our friend Kathy whose "dinner" date turned out to be free Happy Hour hors d'oeuvres.

Usually we laughed at the stories. Sometimes we cried. But we were never bored.

It was during one of our dinners, at Redamak's, a little hamburger place on Lincoln Avenue in Chicago, while we were recounting our latest adventures, that the proverbial light bulb went on.

Hey, we thought, if we've got so many stories, and our friends have so many stories, other people must have them, too. If we love to talk about them, share them, analyze them, hash them, rehash them, and try to make some sense out of them, other people might, too.

That's how we got the idea for a newspaper column that would let people, in their own words, tell their own stories about love and romance. About making up and breaking up. About happy endings and broken hearts.

Not an advice column. Just a place where people could share their tales of falling in love and falling out of love and starting all over again. Where they could say, "This is what happened to me. . . ."

That same night we hit on a name. *Tales from the Front* seemed perfect. Love is a battlefield, sure. But it's also a time, like war, when everything is more exciting. You know the way men love to sit around telling war stories? Well, we wanted a column that would be a communal bonfire where today's soldiers, the ones engaged in romantic battles, could swap love stories.

The logo seemed to fit. Cheryl sketched the heart behind barbed wire on a napkin. That was in November 1984. The column began in March 1985. It was nationally syndicated a year later.

We've learned so much from our readers. We learned that there are lots of terrific marriages out there. So many of our letters recount romantic first dates or serendipitous meetings and then end: "And that was thirty years and three kids and six grandchildren ago. And we still hold hands in the movies." We've also learned that there are a lot of lonely people. Many readers say that the column makes them feel better. It makes them realize that they're not the only women who haven't had a date in a year or they're not the only nice guys who have been dumped for jerks.

We like to think we have a special rapport with our readers. They keep in touch with us. They let us know how their romances are progressing or deteriorating. We're happy to say that dozens of couples who wrote us about the first glorious days of their romances are still together. Our youngest letter writer was a thirteen-year-old girl who had just had her heart broken by a fifteen-year-old brute. She was sure she would never love again. Our oldest was an eighty-seven-year-old woman who was juggling three boyfriends. Our longest letter was a handwritten saga from a heartsick young man that covered twenty-two pages—both sides—of a legal pad. We have a nun in Iowa who writes us and a woman who says she laminates our columns. Maybe she uses them as placemats.

The columns were the inspiration for this book. But as we read through them, certain themes just jumped off the pages. After we read the eleventh letter from women who were rejecting men on the basis of their ties, their two-toned shoes, or their high-pitched laughs, we saw a trend: Ms. Picky-Picky-Picky was born. When we heard from men and women who were living with unpacked boxes in their living rooms, keeping their lives on hold until they got married, the Carton Complex took shape.

All of our stories are true. The only things we change are names and, sometimes, occupations. If the people in them seem real, it's because they are. We talk about them all the time. If you eavesdropped on one of our conversations, you'd hear us chatting about Candy and Norman, who met at a video dating service, or Muffy and Jake, the ultimate yuppie and the working-class stiff, or Warren and Marie, the couple that took twenty-two years to finally get together. They've all become friends of ours. And we hope, as you read, they'll become your friends, too.

May 1987

1

Do You Come Here Often? Or How People *Really* Meet

It's a whole new ball game out there. Boys are still meeting girls, girls are still meeting boys, but now they're doing it at supermarket singles nights. They're signing up for video dating services. They're placing personal ads in the Lonely Hearts pages. They're taking classes that teach them how to turn chance meetings into close encounters. They're giving BYOB parties where the B isn't booze, it's an old boyfriend.

Video Dating

How far will you go in your quest for Mr. or Ms. Right? (Mr. or Ms. All Right? Mr. or Ms. Tolerable?) Are you up to joining a video dating service? Plenty of people are. Meet Candy.

Candy is short, but she always knew she wanted a tall husband. Still, the people at the video dating service she joined kept trying to match her with short men.

"I don't *like* short men," she told them. "I want tall. When I'm with a short man we look like Munchkins."

"But this one's a doctor," the video matchmaker told her. "When he stands on his wallet, he's six feet tall."

Candy wasn't buying. She stuck to her guns and finally Norman, a six-footer, came up on tape. To make a long, improbably romantic story short, Candy married Norman and today—this is the truth—they run their own video dating service.

There are no illusions in the video dating game. You can just happen to be in a bar. You can pretend to wander into a singles party. But when you sign up for a video dating service and plunk down anywhere from $150 (for senior citizens) to more than $1,500 (for VISP—Very Important Single Person—treatment), you're telling the world, or at least all those strangers who are going to view your tape: "I'm alone and I don't like it."

Before you take that step, let's give you a preview of what will happen should you decide to take the plunge. At least here's what happened the day we paid a visit to Candy and Norman's video dating service.

First of all, we sat down in the viewing room. There was a little static,

---

then the first tape came on. A blond man fills the TV screen. An honest-to-goodness hunk. A commodities broker with a dimpled chin. He shifts in his chair, he leans back, he leans forward, he clasps his knees, he looks around, a self-conscious smile flickering on and off. He's talking to the camera and to Candy who's off-camera, playing talk-show hostess. ("It's a beautiful Saturday afternoon. What are you going to do?" she or Norman will frequently ask the tape makers to warm them up. "Laundry," some reply.) Now she asks the hunk, "What attracts you to a woman?"

"I like someone who likes to laugh," he says, loosening up. "Someone who likes to have fun, who says what she feels." (It turns out that the hunk has found his fun-loving, outspoken, happy-go-lucky mate. His membership is now on hold.)

Next tape.

It's a heavy-machine operator, wearing a plaid shirt. His face is strained; his eyes dart. Norman asks him what's the first thing he notices about a woman if he's at, say, a cocktail party.

Tough question. The strong-but-silent type thinks and thinks and finally says, "Her waist."

Next tape.

Now here's the service's oldest client, Mel, a seventy-one-year-old widower. He says he appreciates sincerity in a woman. He also appreciates youth. Mel is looking for a nice widow or divorcee between forty-five and fifty-five. He doesn't want a thing to do with Georgia. At sixty-eight, she's the service's oldest female client. She's had one date since she joined, but she's not giving up. She comes in once a week to see what's cooking. She makes a day of it: lunch downtown, a movie, a little chit-chat with Candy and Norman. She has redone her video tape three times.

But love does come to some clients, and so does marriage. Just look at Candy and Norman. They're their own best advertisement.

How-to-Meet-People Courses

On any given night, while a chunk of the singles population is happily exchanging life stories, casually brushing hands, jotting down phone numbers, making fun-fun-fun plans for later, there is another group sitting on hard folding chairs, earnestly taking notes on "how to make the first move" and "how to turn a brief meeting into something more significant." They've signed up for one of those How-to-Meet-People courses at a Y or a community center. In other words, how to pick someone up. How to elevate an elevator ride into Kismet. How to turn the wait to get your tangerines weighed into an endless string of tomorrows.

But all that comes later. At the beginning, this specific group—nine men and four women, including an attorney, an engineer, an artist, a computer programmer, a respiratory therapist, and a checker at a K mart—is being asked to share their best and worst experiences meeting people.

There are some happy stories. One woman tells of following a man into one art museum in Amsterdam and out of another. She wound up spending a glorious, culturally enriching week with him.

A college professor who describes himself as "a scientist, philosopher, and poet" recalls a stimulating conversation with a stranger in an airport. Nothing came of it—they were just planes passing in the night, so to speak—but he seems satisfied.

Then there are the not-so-happy tales. The respiratory therapist—she's taking the class for the second time—once asked a colleague to join her after work for margaritas. The night was a sloshy success, at least for her. But when she repeated the invitation several weeks later, he turned her down with a flat and final, "No."

A salesman tells about the time he thought he was ready to close the deal with a woman in a bar. He asked her if she'd like to come to a little party he and some of his buddies were having. She told him the bar was closing in five minutes and he'd better have a better line than that one. He didn't.

The engineer describes walking along the street one day and spotting an attractive woman. She passes him by and then turns around and seems to be following him. He decides to test her. There's a cocktail lounge just ahead, so he walks in and sits down at the bar. Sure enough, she walks in right after him and takes a seat at a little table for two. "I figured I had it made," he says. He orders a drink. She does likewise. And then he saunters over to her, a big grin on his face, and says, "May I join you?" And she says, "No, I'm waiting for my husband." He has to turn around and walk *aaalllll* the way back to the bar. A distance now longer than a football field.

So much for the past. How about the future? The course's instructor is all in favor of a catchy opening line or clever ploy and she encourages creativity. For example, "Cathy," the comic strip character, once spotted an attractive man in a restaurant and sent him an order of potato salad. That kind of thing.

But these first moves can leave you wide open to rejection, so the instructor advises having some excuses handy in case your potato salad is not met with a returning order of cole slaw.

"Tell yourself, 'So what? He must be gay,' or 'Who cares? She's probably married,' " the instructor advises. "It's a healthier way to deal with rejection than thinking, 'I knew it, I'm ugly,' or 'This proves it, everybody hates me.' "

Ah, the games people play when they're searching for romance.

Bring-Your-Old-Boyfriend Parties

But of course you're not ugly and everybody doesn't hate you and sooner or later you're going to find a perfectly presentable person. And then sooner or later you're going to dump that perfectly presentable person. Not that there's anything wrong with the PPP, it's just that you're bored, you're ready to move on, you're restless, or you've found someone better—smarter, sexier, richer, funnier, cuter.

But wait a minute! There's still a lot of life left in that old PPP. That PPP is really too good to be thrown back into the sea. That PPP should be recycled.

And that's how the BYOB (Bring-Your-Old-Boyfriend) party was born. We all know that one man's meat is another man's poison. Therefore it follows that one woman's reject could quite possibly be another woman's snuggle in front of a cozy fire or date for New Year's Eve, or even her marching partner for a hike up the aisle.

It's with that thought in mind that one group of women has been holding BYOB parties pretty much nonstop since 1970. They've hosted Friday night get-togethers, Sunday brunches, Tuesday evening discussion groups. They've even toasted the spring equinox together.

"The parties were a product of the seventies," says Teresa, fifty, one of the original party goers. "It was exciting to be single in those days. We all had stars in our eyes. We asked everyone we knew for the names of eligible men. We'd go up and down the list of country club members looking for them. They had to be rich, handsome, educated, professional, and available. They didn't have to be tall—we had some short women. And then we did a social Dun & Bradstreet on them. We checked them out. No bachelors, we didn't trust anyone who had never been married. Only divorced men and widowers. And no wife beaters. One really great-looking guy was rejected because he once pushed his wife down the stairs. We'd have black-balling sessions and one 'no' vote was all it took."

The women went so far to find the right men that they even chased cars. One aggressive member spotted a Rolls-Royce driven by a super-stud. There was no one sitting in the passenger's seat so she followed until she could jot down the license plate number. Then she got a lawyer who knew a policeman who owed him a favor to trace it. The man received an exploratory phone call—no, he was not married—and an invitation.

Back then, the men ranged from thirty-five to forty-five, the women from thirty to thirty-five. The women chipped in $15 apiece to buy the food and the men were required to bring a bottle of booze.

"You can't believe the stuff we got," recalls Teresa. "Magnums of champagne, vintage wine, double bottles of scotch. Everyone was classy. The men all had real suntans and the women had real diamonds from their first marriages."

Of the original group of twenty-five women, every single one of them has married, at least once. Many of them met their husbands at the parties. Some of the women are back on the market again, and the parties are still going strong.

But now everyone is fifteen years older. The women are between forty-five and fifty; the men between fifty-five and sixty-five—and up.

How up? Listen to this. Before a recent party, one of the hostesses was phoning the men who hadn't RSVPed to see if she could strong-arm them into attending. She called the home of one gentleman and a woman answered the phone. (This is not all that unusual.) When she explained the reason for the call, the woman said, "When are you women going to leave my brother alone? He's seventy-one years old and he's been in a nursing home for seven months." It was time to update the master invitation list.

As the group gets older, this kind of response becomes more and more common. Carla, another founding member, was recently making follow-up calls when a housekeeper answered. Carla asked her if her boss was planning on making the party. The housekeeper said she doubted it, he had just died.

"I know it sounds awful," says Carla, "but I started to laugh to myself. I've heard every excuse in the world, but I thought this one was a little drastic."

Not one to take a housekeeper at her word, Carla looked the man up in the obituary column to make sure he was really dead. He was. Another good one gets away.

Adult Education Courses

Let's face it. Everyone's ideas about dating are probably set somewhere in Archie and Veronica Land: high school. Nobody's married. At worst they're going steady. You walk along the halls and there are hundreds of people coming at you and all of them are single. The same thing is pretty much true in college.

It's no wonder then that once people get out in the real world, when they're lonely they automatically think of school. Night school. Adult education courses. "Take a course and meet women," your friends tell you. "Take a course and meet men."

It doesn't always work. One woman signed up for a course called "How to Read an Annual Report." There were six women enrolled. But still in all, you can learn a lot in night school. Ed is an example of a guy who learned what not to do—never, ever—when you meet someone you like.

Ed is twenty-nine, a buyer for a hospital, and he signed up for a ten-week course in salesmanship. He was immediately attracted to Megan.

"You know how it is," he says. "There are certain intangibles that just draw you to someone." In this case, the intangibles included "a wholesome Irish face, intelligence, no apparent emotional baggage, and a positive attitude."

Nevertheless, Ed did not make his move until the last week of class. Then he invited Megan for coffee.

"We talked for an hour," says Ed. That part sounds good. But there was something strained about the conversation. Megan works in a high school and Ed couldn't steer the conversation away from it. They spent

---

sixty minutes on curricula, detention, and assemblies. "I was ready to grab her and say, 'What do you do outside of school?' " But of course he didn't.

The next night he called and asked her out. Sorry. She was going out of town during spring vacation. When she returned after the holiday, flowers were waiting from Ed. She never called to thank him.

"I wasn't sure she had my work or home phone numbers," says Ed. (How enormous is the human capacity for self-deception? you wonder. How deep is the ocean? How high is the sky?) So Ed waited a couple of days and called again. Megan's roommate answered and wouldn't let him talk to her.

"It wasn't like, 'She's not here.' It was like, 'She's not here and I don't know when she's coming back and never call again!' "

Ed says his instincts told him to give up.

Then Ed, ever a glutton for self-improvement, signed up for another class, a speech class that meets on Saturday mornings. He arrived a little early for the first one and so did Estelle. They chatted and then bumped into each other again after class in the library. Ed asked if she'd like to have lunch.

Would she!

"It was like a job interview," says Ed. "She wanted to know everything about my personal life. Then she told me her whole life story. What it basically came down to was that she was looking to get married—tomorrow. She said she had nothing in her apartment. That was why she was in the library. She was checking out some pictures to cover her walls. She said she was looking for someone with conservative values and then she grabbed my hands and said, 'You have such nice, soft hands.' I thought, 'Come on.' "

It gets worse.

"We're sitting there and she says, 'Why don't you move your chair closer?' and 'Why don't you order this?' and 'Why don't we do this and that together?' We finished lunch and walked to our cars. The teacher had given us the names and phone numbers of everyone in the class and Estelle grabbed my hands again and said, 'You have my number, don't hesitate to use it.'

"I'm thinking, all we did was have lunch and she's making this whole big deal out of it. And then all of a sudden I saw myself in this woman. I thought, 'Do I come on that strong? Is that what I did with Megan?' All *we* did was have coffee. I had no business sending her flowers. I barely knew her. No one wants to be clobbered with instant commitments."

The week went by and Ed did not call Estelle. The next Saturday, he walked into class and "it was like I was going to be tarred and feathered because I hadn't called. I told her, 'I never said I'd call.' She said, 'But you knew I wanted to go out with you,' as though that should have been enough. We wound up sitting on opposite sides of the room."

That's not the worst of it. The worst is that the class had eight more weeks to go.

Personal Ads

For some people, personal ads are a dirty little secret. One woman— 32, SWF, prof, intell, attr.—says it's the dating equivalent of Alcoholics Anonymous. You do it, you just don't talk about it.

Rhonda has no such hang-ups. She's an advertising copywriter, thirty-one, five-feet-five inches and 238 pounds—down from her personal high of 295. She uses the lonely hearts ads to meet men and she's always careful to call herself "Rubenesque" when she lists her attributes. Even so, some men—especially those who flunked Art History 101—are frequently unprepared for her.

She placed an ad one day and arranged to meet Tom, a medical technician, in front of a cozy little restaurant. This was after a nice letter and a warm, friendly half-hour talk on the phone. She said she would be wearing a white silk suit. He said he'd be the one in the blazer. When she arrived, he was leaning against the building, reading a book.

"He looked up and then turned away as though I couldn't be the one he was waiting for," recalls Rhonda. "I went up and said, 'Are you Tom?' I've never seen such a look of total disappointment on anyone's face. All the color drained out, as if his worst nightmare had just come true."

Before we go any further, let's get one thing perfectly clear: Tom has never been a finalist in a Rob Lowe look-alike contest. Not even close. Tom Cruise can sleep nights.

"He was losing his hair and developing a paunch," says Rhonda. "His skin was blotchy like he had had a recent bout of acne." Tom was not particularly well dressed either. He was not a custom-made guy. Cash and carry is more like it.

Their date, needless to say, was a disaster. Tom was hostile and spoke only when spoken to. And then he responded with one-word answers. The night had all the charm of an audit by the IRS.

"I was home by seven-thirty. At least I didn't have to cook," Rhonda says.

Not all the men who responded to Rhonda's "Rubenesque" ad were turned off by her weight. Some were positively turned on by it. That turned *her* off. "I was sitting in my car kissing one of these guys once, and he grabbed me by the waist and said, 'You're such a nice, fat girl.' That was the beginning of the end for me. He didn't care anything about me and what I'm like. All he wanted was someone soft and mushy."

Rhonda's not easily discouraged. In one summer, she went through thirty-one men, all of whom she met through personal ads, all of whom she calls "social parasites." They included one fellow who had a whole harem of fat women, six or seven of them. He'd get around to each of them once a week. What a guy!

Then Rhonda signed up with a dating service that plays your audio tape over the telephone to interested parties. She made her tape and received three responses. One of them contained a picture.

"It wasn't the most impressive picture I've ever seen or the most impressive letter either, but it showed a warmth and wit that touched me. I called him, we met, and we've been dating for ten months now. I'm certain he had some barriers to cross as far as my weight was concerned. And I had to make a few adjustments in my standard of what I considered attractive. . . ."

Such as?

"Well," she says, "he's kind of a nerd. A real Jordache jeans person. He wears a maintenance man key chain that clips on to his belt. He bought one for my son, too. I always envisioned myself with someone who was more yuppie. He doesn't drive a BMW, he has a Nissan Sentra.

He doesn't belong to the fancy health club; I don't think he even knows where it is. He's a working-class guy and proud of it. And I'm happy with him. If it goes on forever, it would be wonderful."

The Blind Date

This may well be known as the decade that invented the supermarket singles night. "It's better than the bars," says one habitué. "Death is better than the bars," says her fern-weary friend. It's a night when all the normal shopping patterns go out the electric door: Everyone wears a name tag and no one fills his cart with generic brands, roach spray, or toilet paper. The store usually helps the mood by putting out snacks from the four basic food groups: wine coolers, lite beer, imported cheese, and gourmet chili. And by the time the produce gets reduced, some desperate people have written "still available" on their name tags.

This may also go down in history as the decade that invented the dating application form. Sure it sounds silly, but the truth is we all enter into relationships with virtual strangers. The woman behind the Avis counter knows more about our dates than we do. You know how it is. You can be dating someone for weeks before you find out he or she can't digest spicy food. Or hates foreign films. Or insists on sleeping with the windows open. Or drinks buttermilk. Or calls dogs "doggies." Or tells racist jokes. At this moment you could be saying "I love you" to someone who eats Sugar Smacks for breakfast and you don't even know it.

One woman dated a man for more than a year before she learned that he had an overwhelming fear of dentists and hadn't been to one in six years. She was shocked to learn that he routinely overcame his toothaches with swigs from a bottle of bourbon. How was it possible he had kept such a crucial bit of information to himself? "Well," she says lamely, "we never discussed dental hygiene." A dating application form could have taken care of that.

So much for the high-tech ways of meeting. (Have we left out bumper sticker singles clubs? It's just a variation on the old "Honk If You're Horny" theme.) When it comes right down to it, people are meeting the same way they always did: blind dates.

Blind dates are like anchovies. There are about a dozen people in the world who really love anchovies and the rest of the population lifts them gingerly off the salad. Eric is a lifter. He thinks a good blind date is like an amiable divorce. Doesn't exist. No such animal. A contradiction in terms.

How did he come to hold such a cynical opinion? Meet Nicole.

Cindy, a mutual friend, fixed them up. Cindy explained that Nicole, her sorority sister, needed a date for a formal dance. But Nicole was no loser. No, indeed. She was a pom-pom girl, very pretty, tall, with blond hair. Eric was also tall. It sounded perfect. He was primed for a good time. "I'm a little bit of a romantic," he says. "I kind of let a picture of the night develop in my head."

Eric picked up Nicole at her dorm and before the dance they went to a pre-party party. It was at this point that she told him, "I was up all night studying for a test. I'm not sure this is going to be very much fun."

Just what Eric wanted to hear. It had the same effect on him as a doctor saying, "This will only hurt for a minute."

The dance was at a fancy hotel. It started off with a fancy meal and

Eric thought it was going pretty well. During dessert he chatted with his other table partners for a few minutes. Then he turned back to Nicole.

"Her head was resting on the table. Motionless."

Eric tapped her on the back.

Nicole rose back up slowly and said, "Sorry. Maybe I'll wake up if we dance."

So they did. Eric noticed that she was dancing at a weird angle away from him and that she never looked at him. She was smiling and dancing vivaciously, but she seemed totally unaware that she had a partner out there.

"I realized she was kind of fixated on somebody off to the side. And then I realized she was staring at herself in the mirrored walls and watching herself dance."

Perhaps that was acceptable behavior, thought Eric. She was, after all, a pom-pom girl.

While the band took a break, the young couple walked out to the lobby and Nicole went to the ladies' room. She came out half an hour later.

Finally, finally, the end of the evening arrived and Eric took Nicole home. She invited him in and suddenly became quite chatty. She told him all about her family and showed him some pictures. Then she picked up another photo and said, "This is my boyfriend. He's in France."

It's not like Eric had been falling in love or anything, so he wasn't crushed. But he was annoyed. If she had told him sooner that she had a boyfriend, he says his expectations would have been different. He could have just relaxed. Not tried so hard to make a good impression.

Eric kind of shook his head and walked to the door to leave. And that's when he said the sentence that ends most first-and-last dates:

"Thank you, I had a very nice time." And that's when Nicole said the sentence that shall be forever burned into Eric's heart: "Well, I'm glad one of us did."

And that's one reason why today, at the ripe old age of twenty-two, Eric says, "I'm pretty jaded about women."

Kelly is pretty jaded about men. She feels the same way about blind dates that Eric does. She just came at it from a different direction.

Kelly has a friend Sally who thinks everyone should be married. "She thinks singleness is a disease that should be eradicated, especially before her husband catches it," explains Kelly. So in order to help stamp out this epidemic, Sally made Kelly her project, fixing her up with a series of men.

"If she tells you she *knows* the man, that means she has seen him at least once," explains Kelly. "If she tells you that the two of you have a lot in common, it means you're both breathing."

The first fix-up was Ken. He was in his mid-forties, a nice match for Kelly, who is thirty-six, recently divorced, and the mother of three teenage boys. Ken came to the door carrying a large plastic bag.

"I didn't know if I should open it or if he was handing it to me so I could throw it out," says Kelly. "I know it's been a while since I've been single, and I don't expect today's American male—especially one I've never met before—to bring me flowers or candy, but I was totally unprepared for a Hefty bag."

She opened it. It was filled with white plastic microwave-proof dishes. Service for twelve. Some dishes were stamped "Swanson," others "Pillsbury." Ken is in plastics. He took Kelly for a drink. They talked mostly about plastics. New plastics. Old plastics. Research in plastics. Breakthroughs in plastic. It was a long night.

Hal, thirty-nine, was next. He's a stockbroker from California who frequently does business in Kelly's town. He didn't have any bags with him, just an article about himself from an aerobics magazine that listed his various glorious accomplishments.

"He liked numbers," recalls Kelly. "He would say things like, 'How many phone calls do you make a day? How long is the average one? What are your kids' grade-point averages?' He recorded all of his aches and pains, the time of the day he had them, how long they lasted, when they went away."

He also corresponded with the U.S. Army. It seems he had signed up with the Army's Run For Your Life Program and he sent them weekly logs of how many miles he had run and his general physical condition, which was obviously pretty good. Kelly and Hal went to dinner. He told her he would call the next time he was in town and that she should feel free to call him in L.A. But he asked her to be a little careful about the sort of message she left with his secretary. Hal, it seemed, was only single when he was on the road.

Kelly's final fix-up was with Tank, forty-eight, one of those rare males who does bring women candy: he handed her eight Hershey's kisses in a Baggie closed with a twist tie.

As he drove to the movies, Tank told Kelly he had prepared a list of hypothetical situations to test their compatibility. Before he began, he asked her if she knew what an analogy was.

"I'm an English teacher," Kelly told him. "I teach composition."

Assured they were on the same wave length, Tank then explained he was thinking of an analogy: Kelly was a tomato and her three children were her seeds.

If he had been in her creative writing class, he would have just flunked.

Later that night, her youngest son, with the divine wisdom of children, said it all. "Mom," he asked, "How could you go out with a man named Tank?" Kelly had no answer.

Sally made it a point to check up on her handiwork. She asked Kelly how the dates worked out. "Not so great," Kelly told her. "Well," said Sally. "They *seemed* nice. They were single."

Other horror stories of Blind Dates from Hell:

• TIPPI: "I opened my door to a six-foot-five monster, beer in hand, spitting his cigarette on my doorstep. We went to a popular college bar. Every single person there knew of him. He introduced me as his girl-friend and tried to hang all over me. Then he hurled plastic beer pitchers into the crowd. I told him he was the most repulsive human being I had ever met. He agreed."

• RYAN: "We had a very nice time until we got to her apartment. She had voodoo things all over the place. She said she loved Haitian art, but there was more than just some art hanging around. I couldn't wait to get out of there. I figure I've got enough problems in my life. I don't need someone getting mad at me and sticking pins in a doll."

• MOLLY: "He told me he had traveled extensively in the Orient so we made plans to go to a nearby Chinese restaurant. He insisted on ordering because of all his travels: one order of beef chop suey. He said it would be plenty for the two of us. No appetizers, nothing. The whole dinner took twenty minutes. Then he walked me home. I went upstairs and fixed myself something to eat."

• PAUL: "I asked her what she wanted to do, thinking she would say, 'Let's meet for a drink and talk.' Instead she said, 'Oh, I'd like to see *42nd Street.*' We're talking about a first date that'll cost a hundred dollars give or take. And who knows if we'll even see each other again?"

• DIANE: "I had a blind date and we went out to lunch. I sat across the table from him for an hour and when it was all over, the best thing I could say about him was that he has all his own hair."

• FRED: "I went out with an insurance saleswoman and she treated the date like a sales call on an important client. She told dirty jokes, which I guess you have to do if you want to be one of the guys. She kept talking about actuarial tables. At one point I told a joke and she actually slapped me on the shoulder. At the end of the night, I was too honest to say I had a good time. I just shook her hand."

• ELAINE: "We went out to dinner. Somewhere between his ex-wife stories and my entrée, I politely excused myself to use the ladies' room— which happened to be six miles away, at my apartment."

• PETER: "It was a date for a black tie dinner. I work at a very fashionable department store and we were going to be sitting with the chairman of the company and all the senior executives. I picked her up and she was wearing some kind of a hand-crocheted shawl and a skirt that looked like one of those poodle skirts from the fifties. The next day, someone who had been at the party called me up and started to bark."

Have we given you the impression that the only good blind date is one that's over? We didn't mean to. Meet Eloise. She opened her door to a man dressed in a blue stocking cap, black slacks, white shirt, brown sweater, and a red polyester jacket that had "Sy" monogrammed over the left breast. He was short and overweight by a good twenty pounds. It was about as unpromising a start as a date can have.

Yet as the evening wore on, Eloise realized what a rare person Sy was. "He was honest, he was scared, more so maybe than I was, not pushy. He told dumb jokes and laughed a lot at himself. He had a positive attitude about life and a fun-loving nature. And I have never felt so at home with someone in all my life."

Eloise has never regretted saying "yes" when Sy asked if he could see her again. They became friends, then lovers, and now they're husband and wife.

The Opening Line

You spot someone attractive. She looks available, at least no one's stapled to her side. You catch her eye. You give her your sexiest look. Maybe a hint of your boyish smile. She seems interested. Definitely. But you can't stand there forever just grinning. You've got to say something. What?

Opening lines are the hardest part of a relationship. (Closing lines are easy: "Have a nice life," "I hope you die," "I hate your meatloaf," "I lied. You're a lousy lover," "You look just like your mother," "You're not tipsy, you're drunk," "I make more money than you do," all come to mind.) But opening lines are a little more difficult—even though they've been around ever since Eve turned to Adam, batted her baby blues and said, "Would you like a bite?" How many times have you heard:

- Say, don't I know you from somewhere?
- Come here often?
- What's your sign?

Those are the most common opening lines. Here are some of the worst:

- Pam, an assistant manager of a restaurant and bar in Battle Creek, Michigan, a.k.a. Kelloggsville, says that one evening she was asked, "What's your favorite kind of cereal?" Not even Snap, Crackle, or Pop could score with that line.

- Cathleen says in one night in one bar she heard the following lines: "You sure like to guzzle that wine" and "You look like a mountain climber." She left before anyone spotted her nibbling the nachos and had a chance to say, "Boy, can you pack it away!"

Worst lines also include anything that begins with "You remind me of my . . ." Fill in the blank with mother, father, priest, first wife, first husband, kindergarten teacher, parole officer, or therapist.

Best lines are harder to categorize. A young man pointing up at the stars and sighing, "They're beautiful, aren't they? Someday I'd like to take you there" did it for Louise. Of course she was only thirteen at the time. Rusty, who frequents strip joints, is turned on by directness: "If you've got the money, I've got the time" or "Buy me a cocktail. I haven't had my quota yet."

There's nothing wrong with the honest approach: "I like your smile. Will you have dinner with me?" "You smell good. What's that perfume you're wearing?" "Do you always jog on this path?" "Wait a second, you left your umbrella." None of them may win awards, but under the right circumstances, any of them can do the trick.

It's really quite simple. When the right person says it, "Excuse me, you're standing on my foot" can set your pulse racing.

The truth is, no matter how difficult it is to meet people, no matter how many blind dates you have to endure, no matter how many "Gee, did anybody ever tell you you look like . . ." lines you have to hear, no matter how many courses you have to take or ads you have to answer, eventually you will meet someone. It's inevitable. The question is: Who? Meet today's women and men.

2

The Players:
The Women

It was easy in the old days. There were two kinds of women. Those who did. And those who didn't. AIDS is making people more selective, but eventually almost everyone does. So much for the old categories.

Then how *do* you define women these days? How do you put them in slots? Who are today's *real* women? Look around you on the elevator. Assess your coworkers. Stare into the bathroom mirror. We think you'll see these basic types.

There's the Telephone Answering Machine Junkie. You know her. You may even be her. She turns on her answering machine before she throws out the garbage. Her message sounds something like this: "Hi, I'm in the shower right now, but if you leave your name and number, I'll get back to you just as soon as I towel off."

There's the Die-hard. She doesn't give up. She never says uncle. "Over" is not in her vocabulary. She stands by her man, even when her man is standing next to someone else.

There's Ms. Rumpelstiltskin. Remember the old fairy tale about the princess who wove gold from straw? Well, there are a lot of modern princesses out there doing the exact same thing. They take the most casual comments from men and build a future on them. Example: He says, "Thanks, I had a nice time." She hears, "I love you. I want you to bear my children."

There's Miss Hickory-Dickory-Dock. Her biological clock is ticking so loudly it keeps her up nights. She's dying to get married. She's always looking over your shoulder to see if an available man is walking by. Her apartment is a reflection of all the guys who have passed through her life. There's a Mr. Coffee and she doesn't even drink coffee. A pair of cross-country skis left over from a brief fling with a superjock. "How to Talk Football to Men" is her bedtime reading.

There's Ms. Picky-Picky-Picky. No man is good enough for her. She dismisses men because they laugh too loudly, use the expression "okey-dokey," or wear lime green. She walks into a party and determines in ten seconds if her future husband is there. He never is. She's searching for someone with the looks of a young Laurence Olivier and the brains of an old Albert Einstein.

There's Fate's Fool. She consults astrologists, psychics, palm readers, handwriting analysts, and Shirley MacLaine. She looks for signs and omens everywhere. She finds them. If the same man boards her bus twice in the same month, it's destiny. Three times and it was Meant to Be.

The Telephone Answering Machine Junkie

"Hi, this is Susie and I'm so sorry I can't talk right now. But if you leave your name and number and a brief message, I'll return your call just as soon as I can. Now wait for the beep. And have a nice day!"

• No seriously single woman is without a telephone answering machine.

• Upon arriving home after work, no seriously single woman removes her coat without first playing back her messages.

• No seriously single woman, upon finding *no* messages, has not called a friend and asked her to call to check whether her machine is broken.

• No seriously single woman's happiness is not at times contingent upon the blinking of that little red light.

Most seriously single women are Telephone Answering Machine Junkies. They're addicted to a fake-wood box.

You think you're immune? You think you can take your answering machine or leave it? You think it's just a convenience, in the same category as hot rollers and Soup for One? Sucker. Answer the following questions:

1. Have you ever stayed home watching "Saturday Night Live" with your answering machine turned on so no one would know the *real* state of your social life?

2. Have you ever called up a friend and played your really good messages for her so that the two of you could savor them together?

3. Have you ever realized a relationship was over when your boyfriend asked you to walk out of the room before he turned on *his* machine to play back *his* messages?

4. Have you ever recorded favorite messages off your answering machine and onto a tape recorder so that you could play them back at your leisure, kind of like an audio diary?

5. Have you ever been standing at the bus stop when you realized you forgot to turn on your machine, so you turned around and went home to hit that switch?

6. Do you find yourself calling in for your messages regularly? (And do you make it a point to carry loose change so that you can call in from pay phones when you're going to be out?)

7. Do you find yourself panicking while your answering machine is being repaired?

8. If your apartment was on fire, would you turn on your answering machine before you ran out the door?

Did you answer *yes* to at least half the questions? Welcome to Telephone Answering Machines Anonymous. You have friends here.

Marla is very creative with her answering machine. She counts her hang-ups and interprets them like tea leaves.

One night she was determined to figure out who had left a particular hang-up. She knew it hadn't been the guy she was dating because she had made a point of telling him she was taking a Chinese cooking class after work. It wasn't her mother—she was on vacation in the Bahamas. It couldn't have been her girlfriends because they know how much she hates it if they don't leave a message.

"I could hear noise in the background before the hang-up and by straining my ears and playing it back repeatedly I made out the sound of cars. So I knew it had to be someone calling from an outdoor pay phone. I have this one ex-boyfriend who I could just imagine driving around and impetuously stopping to call me. No one else I know would pull over and do that. I felt this surge of pleasure. It was as if he had left a message saying, 'I take back every mean thing I've ever said to you.' "

With just a little imagination, Marla managed to hear, "I love you. I'll always love you" in the distant rumblings of traffic.

That's one time that Marla's machine made her happy. There have been many other times when it has failed her. Miserably.

"An answering machine kills all fantasy. When you're single, people say, 'Stay active, keep busy, get out of the house.' Before I got my machine, I would do that. And when I got home, I could make myself believe that the phone had been ringing off the hook all day with wonderful calls."

Marla assumed there were invitations to parties, prospective dates, men she had met casually at the grocery store or the cleaners wanting to get to know her better. All kinds of exciting things.

"I can't do that anymore. I might be out on a Sunday from eight-thirty in the morning until ten at night and return to one message from my father. There's no way to put a pretty face on that. And now, with my remote beeper, I can call my machine from anywhere in the world and find out that nobody has called me."

Paula says Mike's answering machine was "almost like a third party in our relationship. In the beginning, whenever I called and it answered, I would listen to his message, which always included a trivia question *he* thought was clever, and then I'd hang up. He went away for two weeks on business and I called every day just to hear his voice. If I was angry with him, I would purposely call and hang up repeatedly because I knew how much he hated that."

In no time at all, Paula learned to use Mike's machine to spy on him. As she said, he was in the habit of changing his trivia question every day, and when the question, something like, "Who won the 1957 World Series?" was the same two days in a row, she knew he had not slept at home the night before.

When Sarah bought her answering machine, she thought it would free her. She'd be able to get out of the house but still get her messages. That's not the way it turned out.

"I had a date for Sunday night with a guy I was going out with, but the plans were very loose. I didn't know what time we were going out or where we were going. I just figured we'd talk sometime during the day. But it was a beautiful summer day and I didn't want to stay home tied to the telephone. So I turned on my answering machine and went to the beach. Every half hour, I found a pay phone and called *my* answering machine to see if he had left a message and then I called *his* answering machine and left him a message. He wound up standing me up, and I was out a pocketful of quarters."

Sometimes when you're wondering what would you ever do without your answering machine, the following response might come to you: "I'd be better off."

The Die-hard

Jill is a Die-hard. She hung in there with a man who could not, would not say "I love you" even though she knew he did.

He would do almost everything else for her. He showered her with candy and gifts. He took her dining and dancing. He bought toys for her three young sons. He'd hide quarters in the house and turn the kids loose to find them. In the summer, he'd stop over nearly every morning before work with a bouquet picked from his mother's garden.

After two months of this first-class treatment, Jill just had to tell Randy she loved him. No response. Time passed and again she told him she loved him. No response.

"You could at least say thank you," said Jill.

So Randy said, "Thank you."

While Randy had an obvious problem saying "love," he had no problem saying "marriage." He said it often. Always in the context of "It's not for me."

Yes, he cared for Jill. Of course he enjoyed her company. But he was not the marrying kind and from time to time he enjoyed the company of other women. As long as he was up-front about it, what was the problem?

"My choices were to accept it or walk away from it," says Jill. She compromised. She lived with it and she hated it. She had no real choice. "I wanted him."

Two years passed and Jill and Randy continued to see each other four times a week. Jill continued to say, "I love you." Randy continued to say, "Thank you."

One night, Jill happened to be at a party without Randy and she met Brian. He wanted to go out with her. Jill thought that was fine and the next day when Randy stopped by, she asked him to start calling before he dropped over because she, too, was planning to see someone else from time to time.

Randy was stunned.

"He sort of started sputtering," says Jill.

And when he could finally spit it out, he said he wasn't interested in sharing her and if that was what she wanted, they could just call it quits right then and there.

"I did point out that he had been seeing other women," says Jill. "He said that was different because I had accepted it and he couldn't."

Good-bye Randy. In the next five days, Jill had three dates with Brian. Randy didn't call and he didn't drop in. He did cruise her neighborhood, however, so she knew that he was thinking about her. But it was a small consolation. She was miserable.

She came home from work one night and crawled into bed. She instructed her oldest son to tell Brian, when he called, that she wasn't feeling well and couldn't talk. As she lay brooding in her bed, she heard the phone ring and she heard her son give the "She doesn't feel well. She can't talk" spiel, not once, but twice. Then the boy came to her and said the man wouldn't hang up. He had to talk to her.

Jill dragged herself to the phone. A loud voice croaked out, "Jill, I love you!" Jill wasn't sure she heard right (Ha!) and she asked the caller to repeat himself. Three times he said it. "I love you . . . I love you . . . I love you." It was Randy.

He came right over and told Jill that he loved her, but he still wasn't the marrying kind. There *were* limits.

"I figured if it were possible to get this man to finally admit his love for me, anything was possible given enough time," says Jill, a true Die-hard.

Anything *was* possible. Randy stopped seeing other women. Jill stopped seeing other men. It took about another year and a threat on Jill's part to move out of town for Randy to propose. He finally asked her to *m-m-m-m-arry* him on a Friday and they did it eight days later.

That was fourteen years ago. Now Jill swears Randy tells her he loves her every single day.

You want to meet another Die-hard? Say hi to Jenny.

The first time Jenny met Adam, he was putting down his ex-girlfriend Tiffany. It was summer, they were at a party, and Jenny overheard him tearing Tiffany to shreds. From what Jenny could make out, it was clear that Tiffany had dumped Adam one time too many and this time he had really had it. Jenny definitely remembers him saying, "I can't stand her."

Now twenty-two-year-old Jenny was attracted to twenty-four-year-old Adam, so those words were music to her ears. They bumped into each other occasionally, and in January, they started to go out. And it was great.

Of course Jenny was curious about the ex-girlfriend. Who isn't obsessed with a current lover's past romances? And Tiffany and Adam had dated off and on for six years. One quarter of Adam's life. The fact that Tiffany had long blond hair and very blue eyes didn't make Jenny any less interested.

Speaking of that blond hair and blue eyes, would you say Tiffany is pretty, Jenny?

"I think she looks trampy," says Jenny, who has short brown hair and thinks of herself as the "down-to-earth type."

But in spite of her curiosity, she never mentioned Tiffany. Once she said to Adam, "I want to ask you something," and he said, "No, I'm not going to go back with Tiffany." "That's not what I was going to ask," Jenny told him.

"I don't think he was completely over her," says Jenny wisely.

One night Adam came over after he had been drinking and he started talking about Tiffany. "He started telling me all these things, terrible things, about her that I just loved to hear. She thinks she's a step above a lot of other people. Her parents shower her with everything. She drives a bright red sports car. I asked, 'How could you have gone out with someone like that?' "

Adam passed it off as some aberration of his youth. He was through with her. That was for sure.

Valentine's Day, a Saturday, was "fantastic." First Adam gave Jenny a dozen long-stemmed red roses. Then they bought steaks and shrimp and cooked themselves a feast. Then . . . well, whatever. They spent the whole weekend together.

Monday was fine. Tuesday was fine. They had plans to go out Wednesday night. Jenny cruised by his house and there, parked right in front, was the bright red sports car.

"I'm thinking, 'I can't believe this.' "

Jenny went home and called Adam. No answer. She was in pretty bad shape the next day at work and her boss sent her home early. Except she didn't go home. She went to Adam's.

"I knocked on his door, it was two in the afternoon, and there he was sound asleep. I said, 'So, did you have a good time last night?' He said, 'Yeah, I got pretty drunk.' I said, 'Oh, who'd you go out with?' He says, 'Some girl.' He wasn't going to come out and say it, so I said, 'Am I getting blown over for Tiffany or what?' "

Adam denied that anything had happened. Tiffany simply happened to stop over. They got drunk. So drunk that they made another date to discuss soberly whatever ground they had covered sloshed. In fact, while Adam was spinning this tale, Tiffany called to check just what time Adam would be picking her up for their "discussion."

Adam walked Jenny to her car, telling her his date with Tiffany was "no big deal and not to worry about it." Then he kissed her and promised her he'd call the minute he got home.

Well, perhaps he hasn't gotten home yet, because that was the last time Jenny ever heard from him.

She did the usual humiliating things: She called him and left messages; she patrolled his neighborhood and even left a letter under his windshield while his car was parked in Tiffany's driveway. The essence of the letter was she was sorry he didn't have the guts to tell her himself that it was over.

Now, let's run the true Die-hard test on Jenny: What if off-again/on-again Tiffany and Adam are on the outs? And Adam calls?

What would you do, Jenny?

"Well, I talked to my girlfriends and they said . . ."

No, Jenny. Not what would your girlfriends do, what would *you* do?

"I think I'm better off staying away from . . ."

Not what do you *think,* Jenny. What would you *do?*

"Oh, God, I'd go out with him again . . ."

And that's how Jenny earned her place in the Die-hard Hall of Fame.

Ms. Rumpelstiltskin

Reflect for a moment on this all-too-common scenario. It's the end of a first date. A couple is standing outside the woman's front door.

He says: "Good night. It was fun. I'll give you a call."

She hears: "I think I'm falling in love with that funny little face of yours. I'll sleep with your name on my lips. I'll dream of you. I'd crawl naked over cracked glass to get to you. You excite me as no other woman ever has. My fingers will dial your number the very second I walk in my house. I must have you."

You are observing Ms. Rumpelstiltskin at work. She can take a "Hi, how's it going?" and weave it into a "Share your life with me, have my children" faster than you can say Mother Goose.

At this very moment, she's doodling wedding invitations on the basis of a couple of dinners. She's deciding whether her pink towels and his blue ones go together or if she's better off registering for beige ones instead, based on what he considers a little recreational sex. She's figuring out the genetic possibilities of giving birth to redheaded children because a carrot-top moved in across the hall. She's telling people she has a boyfriend when all she really has is a date.

Rachel does it relentlessly. She's twenty-seven, a grad student in sociology. She did it on a first date with a guy she hardly knew. They were having one of those early conversations that are really just small talk—Where'd you go to school? Do you like Bruce Springsteen? Why'd you break up with your last girlfriend?—when he mentioned that he had two sisters.

"I found myself thinking, 'Would I have to have both of them in my wedding party?' This is on the first date! And then I started to think actually I'd *like* a man with sisters since I never had one myself."

In her mind, Rachel was already shopping and having lunch with two women she'd never met and probably never will.

She is such a total Ms. Rumpelstiltskin that she doesn't even need a date to go through the routine.

"I went to the dentist the other day because I chipped a tooth. It was a new dentist, young, really handsome, and we were kind of flirting with each other. I developed a huge crush on him, and as I was driving home after the appointment, I was already writing a wedding toast—'Let's lift our glasses to rock candy. It chipped my tooth!' He, of course, was probably just thinking about his next patient, while I had us married."

Do we have to add that Rachel did not hear from her dentist for six months? Then she got a card telling her it was time to get her teeth cleaned.

Miss Hickory-Dickory-Dock

Have you ever noticed that when you get close to some women you hear a kind of tick-tock, tick-tock? They're not terrorists. That's not a

bomb. They're just women—usually in their early thirties—whose biological clocks are ticking so loudly you don't want to sit next to them in
the movies. The ticking keeps these women up at night. They're suffering
from baby lust. They want to be pregnant (and, God willing, married) so
badly that it makes them do irrational things. They stuff pillows under
their sweatshirts to see what they'd look like if they actually were pregnant. They browse through layette shops. They eye the supermarket delivery boy for breeding potential.

They're constantly doing the New Math: "If I walk out of here and
bump into a gorgeous stranger, and he's single, and he says, 'Hi, want to
get married?' it'd take at least a couple of months before I'd say yes. And
then it would take another couple of months to plan the wedding. Listen,
you wait this long, you want to do it right. That's six months right there.
And then we'd want a couple of years to travel—Europe, maybe the
Orient, Africa. I've never been on a safari. And then I'd actually have to
get pregnant. That could take another six months. And then nine months
after that. We're talking three or four years minimum! I'll be old!"

Hickory-Dickory-Docks are constantly wondering why they have not
managed to fulfill their simple biological destiny. Where did they go
wrong? When they get together, that's what they ask.

The other night when the rates went down for the second time, the
phone rang in Lori's house. It was her friend Julia. The two had been
best friends in college, nearly ten years ago. They took the same courses.
They even had the same boyfriend once. Their friendship survived it.
Since then they've moved away and pretty much drifted apart. Lori is a

stockbroker in Chicago. Julia is an accountant in Memphis. But in a crunch, they turn to each other.

That's why Lori knew Julia must have something important to discuss. She's not the kind to chitchat.

"I have news that's going to make you sad," Julia said. "Margie called today. She's pregnant."

Margie was the third in their once-inseparable college threesome.

"I knew you'd get depressed when I told you," Julia continued. "I'm sorry, but I didn't feel like being depressed alone."

The two friends—successful, busy, pretty, and pretty happy in most ways—were jealous. It wasn't fair. They had done everything right. Margie had been the screw-up. How come she was getting all the goodies and they weren't?

They had both been better students than Margie. They had been ambitious; they never missed a class or an assignment. Margie spent her afternoons in bed watching "As the World Turns." She never took an exam on the date it was given. She never handed in a paper on time. She always had an excuse for everything.

After graduation, Julia and Lori immediately enrolled in grad school. They had careers to begin. Life was waiting. They were in a hurry. Margie, on the other hand, took her time *adjusting.* Then she slowly made her way to Virginia. For no good reason. It just kind of sounded like a nice place to live.

After grad school, Lori and Julia found great jobs. They both landed in large, prestigious firms. They were both bringing in big bucks. They had bright futures. They were on the fast track, no question. Every annual review and salary raise confirmed it. Margie, meanwhile, settled for a part-time job selling garden seed. And when she talked to her two friends, she confessed she was really spending more time on her garden than on her seed.

Typical Margie, her friends clucked.

Then, one day a couple of years ago, Margie called to say she was getting married. She wanted her two old college pals to be at the wedding.

They went and they cried. They cried because she looked so beautiful walking down the aisle. And they cried because they had all come so far since college and their lives had taken such different directions.

And they cried because they were jealous. She was getting married and they weren't.

At the wedding, Julia said to Lori, "You wouldn't want the man she married, and you know it. You wouldn't think he was good enough for you. He's not successful enough, and you'd never be happy living in a small town in Virginia."

She reminded Lori that Margie's husband was a hardware salesman. My God, they made three times as much money as he did. At least!

That seemed to help a little. But now there was a new crisis to deal with: the baby.

"I know you're jealous," Julia said. "But you wouldn't trade your career and lifestyle for hers, baby and all, and you know it. Think about where you are in life. Be honest."

So Lori thought about it. And she decided to be really honest. More honest than she'd ever been in her life. And she said, "I'd trade with her in a minute."

Ms. Picky-Picky-Picky

For all their jazzercising, for all their jogging and racquetballing, swimming and weight lifting, many of today's women can be remarkably inflexible. They can touch their toes, all right, they just can't seem to get in touch with reality. Ask one of these women what she wants and she'll tell you with a straight face, "Everything." We call her Ms. Picky-Picky-Picky.

Let's face it. It's hard to find a perfect man these days. But that doesn't stop Denise, the ultimate Ms. Picky-Picky-Picky, from trying.

Denise is thirty-five. She's "tall, thin, very attractive, with dark hair and blue eyes. I dress real sharp. What can I tell you? I hate to sound so cocky, but I can't help it." Personality-wise, she says she's "chatty, open, and honest."

She's also a psychotherapist—specializing in eating disorders—who's been in private practice for five years and pulls in about $30,000 a year. That's supplemented by a healthy chunk every month from her ex-husband. She lives in a four-bedroom house with a pool in a ritzy suburb.

She says she's got "the whole bit," which includes two kids, eleven and six. And now, after being divorced for three years, she has decided she wants to be in love. And she knows just the kind of man she's looking for.

"I want someone with a dynamite personality who's outgoing and witty. He doesn't have to be a Robert Redford, but I wouldn't mind it. He doesn't have to be gorgeous, but I can't stand fat. He has to be bright. I need someone who'll stimulate me.

"And he has to be successful. He doesn't have to make like my ex-husband does, but he does have to make at least $100,000 a year. Five hundred thousand dollars isn't necessary, although I wouldn't mind that either. It isn't just the money. It's the whole concept of someone who's ambitious, aggressive, and wants the finer things in life.

"I want someone who enjoys children, because mine are very important to me, and who's willing to build a relationship with my kids. It's fine if he has kids, but he has to accept that I don't want to have any more. He's got to have a good heart and be romantic and a nice person. And I'm a very strong person, but underneath it all, I'm a softy. I need someone who will see that. Also, I have a tendency to be a little bit self-centered. Usually, I catch it myself, but sometimes I need someone to say, 'Denise, cut it out.' I went with one guy and I couldn't believe the things he took from me. I couldn't respect him."

Once Denise meets this man (This man? This *superman* with psychic powers), she wants to build a relationship with him based on "mutual trust. I want us to feel 100 percent comfortable with each other. I should be able to say whatever I want, be able to not dress up all the time but still look fine to him. We'd travel. Whatever we did together would be fine, but I don't want to stay home seven nights a week either. A nice physical relationship is, of course, important, too. We'd always be there for each other in good times and bad. And we'd have fun. A lot of laughing and joking."

In short, she wants "a soul mate who will not only be my lover but my trusted friend. I do not want just a husband, I want a life partner."

Picky, picky, picky, Denise. But like the women in those L'Oreal commercials, she thinks she's worth it.

"I hate to sound so cocky again, but I feel I'm special and I have something special to offer. Most people who know me agree."

Denise, bless her heart, truly believes that what she wants lies within the realm of possibility, as opposed to an episode of "Fantasy Island." She has some friends, after all, who have the kind of marriage she wants, but alas, not necessarily the kind of husband. One of these husbands is five-foot-five, too short for Denise. The other has put on twenty-five pounds over the last ten years. As this eating disorder specialist says, she "can't do fat."

So in the meantime, she's waiting for that special guy to come along. It's hard to wait. She knows at some point she may have to compromise, but not yet.

Fate's Fool

Nonbelievers can stop reading now. Doubters, move on. This is a tale for those who believe in fate, karma, destiny, psychics, dreams, and things that go bump in the night.

It started in 1964. Annie met Clyde at her sister's wedding. He was the best man; she was the maid of honor. He was twenty-five; she was eighteen. He had a "Butch Cassidy" mustache; she hated it.

"He was very shy and awkward and talking to him was a real effort. I avoided him like the plague," says Annie.

Fast forward. Annie goes to college. Clyde doesn't. Annie is a social worker. Clyde is a manual laborer. They run into each other at family functions. Annie turns away whenever she sees Clyde coming. In addition to all his other faults, he is "weird." He does odd, unforgivable things like collecting exotic cars and motorcycles and reading everything "from law journals to textbooks on calculus and physics."

"I couldn't figure him out and I never understood what he was talking about," says Annie. "Besides, I was too cool to be bothered. I was dating a lot of interesting men in exciting professions. He and I had nothing in common."

In spite of all those "interesting men in exciting professions," there was really nothing much happening in Annie's social life so her sister tried to fix her up with Clyde. She said they were alike in so many ways.

"I was insulted," says Annie.

But her sister kept after her and Annie, who was twenty-five at this point, finally agreed. The date was a disaster. Clyde talked about his many interests—physics, calculus, law. Annie told him he was an egomaniac. That was their last date. They continued to bump into each other, and Annie continued to avoid him.

She was in the midst of falling in and out of disastrous relationships with "fascinating men" when she heard that Clyde had gotten married. She said to herself, "That just goes to show you, there's someone for everyone."

Even weird old Clyde.

Since none of her "fascinating men" were working out, Annie decided to visit a psychic for a little romantic counseling. The woman told her that she would fall deeply in love with "someone who had been on the periphery of my life for many years." But since there was absolutely no one who fit that description, Annie was sure the woman "obviously didn't know what she was talking about."

By now it was 1980 and Annie was thirty-four. She had had plenty of "interesting men in exciting professions" by this time. She had just pulled herself out of "yet another going-nowhere relationship" when she had a dream.

"It was the most wonderful dream," says Annie. "Weird Clyde and I were riding on his motorcycle. We were laughing and talking and I was deliriously happy. I had heard he had gotten divorced, but I never gave him another thought, until this dream. Then I couldn't stop thinking about it. It was so vivid and real and he was so different from the way I had always perceived him. He was so much fun."

So, Annie called Clyde and invited him over for dinner. He was, needless to say, shocked to hear from her. She had, after all, been avoiding him for sixteen years.

Annie was a little shocked herself. Clyde sounded so sexy on the phone. Funny how she had never noticed that before.

When he arrived, she also noticed how "gentle and warm" his brown eyes were. Another fact that had escaped her. When he told her he had heard she had been dating a lot of "interesting people" she blurted out, "better to *be* an interesting person."

It dawned on her that she was talking about him.

Well, you guessed it. They started dating and got married two years ago and they're as happy today as they were in Annie's dream.

Will the Answering Machine Junkie ever unplug her machine? Will Ms. Rumpelstiltskin ever leave her loom? Will the Die-hard ever give up?

Will Ms. Picky-Picky-Picky learn the art of compromise? Will Miss Hickory-Dickory-Dock stop cruising the Layette Department? Will Fate's Fool stop reading her horoscope? Of course they will. Just as soon as they find the right guy. To meet some of their choices, read on.

3

The Players: The Men

If you're a woman, we know you've dated at least one of these men. Remember that guy who left for good the morning after you told him, "I'm beginning to like you a lot"? How about the one who liked you best when you treated him worst? Or the fellow who was so, so, so nice, and so *right* for you . . . only you couldn't quite make yourself fall for him?

If you're a man, no doubt at one time or another you've *been* one of these guys. Remember that woman you adored, even after she said thanks for the trip to Hawaii, but I'm engaged to someone else? Do you ever think about that relationship where you thought you were *lovers* and she told you you were *just friends?*

Meet today's men. They're a complex group, these guys, but a few things are certain. They are *not* walking down the street whistling "Dixie" because there are 4.1 women for every one of them. (Or 2.3. Or 1.8.) They can be just as puzzled as the women (if a little less panicked). Their ticking biological clocks keep *them* from sleeping too. "I don't want to be sixty-five years old and playing catch with my six-year-old," one told us.

You'll meet Mr. Confused. He doesn't understand the rules of the new dating game. He won't say it out loud, but secretly he envies his grandfather, whose wife was selected for him by a cousin in the old country. Mr. Confused has been on dates where he has gotten a dirty look if he doesn't ask to come upstairs. He's been on others where he's gotten a worse look if he does. What's a guy to do? Don't ask him.

He knows where the Nice Guy is coming from. Every woman is the Nice Guy's friend, but none of them look at him with that sizzle that says, "I want you." He's had too many conversations with women who tell him, "There are no nice guys." He feels like saying, *"I'm* a nice guy." He's the great undiscovered man. His day will come.

For now, though, women just keep passing him over for Mr. Gotta Keep Moving On. The better it gets, the faster this one is gone. Most women have met him—or at least seen his taillights. This is the one who comes on like gangbusters, sweeps you off your feet, then disappears over the horizon. Address unknown.

Then there's the Sucker. He also gets the girl. The wrong ones. The ones who leave him high and dry, the ones who have "I'm a heartbreaker, you must be an idiot" written all over their gorgeous bodies—

---

only the Sucker can't see it. And he never learns his lesson, even when all he can find in his pockets after she's through with him is lint.

Mr. Confused

This man doesn't feel the least bit consoled just because the numbers tell him that he can walk into any bar on any night and find ten eligible women. "I still have to go up to one woman," Mr. Confused says. "When they talk about being rejected, women don't realize that men face that same possibility a hundred times in a night, every time they ask someone to dance."

There are Mr. C. representatives in every generation. There's the fifty-year-old man whose wife left him and whose friends tell him he'll be on Easy Street. He doesn't want to be on Easy Street. He wishes he were right back in the living room, sitting on the sofa, reading the paper next to his wife of twenty-five years. There's the twenty-year-old who's burned out after only a few tender years of dating because of the girl he took out who spent the whole evening talking about her *real* boyfriend.

Nor does it seem to get better with practice. Even after he makes the first connection and makes it well, Mr. Confused still feels on thin ice. Take William. Conventional wisdom suggests that William should be having the time of his young life. He's single, he's male, he's got a good job, makes a good living. You wouldn't think he would have much on his mind beyond whether or not to get racing stripes on his next car. But it's not that way. He worries. He doesn't quite understand women, and he doesn't quite feel comfortable with the dating scene.

"The second I walk out the door for the beginning of the date, I am starting to worry about the end of the date," the twenty-nine-year-old told us.

Worry about what?

"I am thinking out the logistics in my head. I picture pulling up to her front door in my car. I picture saying that I'll walk her to her door. I picture the next moment. The issue of should I tell her I'll call her even if I won't. The whole question of whether I should ask her out for the next date at the end of this date or put some space in between."

A few weeks ago William took a woman out on a date. It was a Friday night. They went to see a movie and then they got something to eat. They both had a nice time as far as William could tell. This was their second time out together.

After their first date William had pulled into the circular driveway in front of her apartment building. He got out of the car, walked her about three steps to the front door, told her what a good time he had (he really had) and that he would call (he really would).

"The doorman was watching this whole thing and I could tell he was waiting to see if I was going to kiss her good night," he says. So he didn't.

"That's something I don't think women understand, that it's really hard for a man to know exactly what to do, or what a woman wants or expects. My date probably walked into her building and wondered all the way up in the elevator why I hadn't kissed her good night and if I was going to call—this is assuming she had a good time too and I know she did—but I doubt it crossed her mind that this is an issue that men go over in their minds too."

The second date becomes even a little more complicated.

"Let's say you didn't kiss her good night at the end of the first date,"

William says. "That's fine. Then you go out on the second date and you walk her to her door. Maybe she'll invite you in. But let's say she doesn't. You probably kiss her good night. But believe me, you've thought it out. You've thought about what kind of kiss. About what kind of relationship it might turn out to be."

At the end of William's recent second date, he did give her a kiss good night. He had worked it out in advance. He pulled up in the circular driveway again, but this time he stopped his car just this side of the doorman's line of vision (he assumed the doorman wasn't going to walk outside and turn his head sharply to the right). William gave his date a kiss *in* the car, then got out and walked her to the door. Nothing spontaneous here.

The third date will take place soon.

"Third dates," William says, "can be very tricky. After this one she may invite me up to her apartment. I could tell after the second date that she was about to, but she probably remembered that she had left dirty dishes in the sink or something. This time she will, and then we'll both have different questions in our minds ranging from 'Where should I sit, on the chair or the sofa?' to 'And now what? How long should I stay?' There are no easy answers."

In some ways Mr. Confused is Every Man. While she's wondering, "Is he going to kiss me?" he's thinking, "Should I?" While she is obsessing with her friends, wondering "Will he call me?" Mr. Confused is agonizing over whether Sunday morning is too soon to pick up the phone to contact her again.

Tim became confused when he found himself Suddenly Single one day after his fourteen-year marriage hit the skids. All of a sudden he was thirty-eight and on his own. The world had changed. The last rules of dating he had memorized applied to teenagers. He knew that adults probably did it differently—but he didn't know how.

"Actually, my very first date after my divorce was no problem," Tim says. "The woman started kissing me in a bar. But that kind of luck didn't last long. Between that date and the next quite a bit of time went by and I didn't know what to do."

But Tim was lucky. During that dry spell he went to see *Annie Hall.* His role model for romantic behavior became Woody Allen. And one scene in the movie, especially, became his inspiration.

That's the one where Diane Keaton and Woody Allen are on their first date. Suddenly Allen stops and says, "Gimme a kiss . . . because we're just gonna go home later, right? . . . and . . . there's gonna be all that tension. You know, we never kissed before and I'll never know when to make the right move or anything. So we'll kiss now, we'll get it over with and then we'll go eat. Okay? . . . And we'll digest our food better."

Three weeks after he saw the movie, Tim had a date. They were walking along the street, struggling to make conversation.

"All of a sudden I said, 'Don't move,' " Tim says. "I just stopped and kissed her. It was so awkward, it made me think what a smooth guy Woody Allen really was."

That relationship didn't last forever, but it had its moments. So Tim wound up using the Sudden Kiss Scenario several times after that, until he met the woman he married. And now he is much less confused. He doesn't have to keep up with the rules of dating anymore and worry whether they're becoming obsolete before he's even learned them.

The Nice Guy

Every woman says she wants one. No one really does.

You know the Nice Guy. He's the kind of man every woman wants for a friend. He'll nurse you through your broken hearts, tell you you're too good for that jerk. He's gentle, kind, supportive, and usually without a girlfriend.

He's the one who sends flowers the day you're giving your presentation at work; he's your man when your car is making funny noises. When you need a date for your cousin's wedding, he'll be there with a corsage. And your parents adore him.

The Nice Guy is related to Mr. Confused, but he's got different troubles. Mr. Confused gets the girl, and then can't figure out what to do with her. Mr. Nice Guy never makes it that far. Or else he makes it through about four dates—until she starts pulling away, because deep inside she wants more of "a challenge."

Monroe is a Nice Guy. Three times he has been in love. And three times he has been dumped. Once he was dumped for a tattoo artist. Once he was dumped for a drug addict. And most recently he was dumped for an unemployed nineteen-year-old. Monroe wonders if all women are crazy—or just the ones he bumps into.

He describes himself as a "handsome, loving, and sensitive person with a bright future ahead of me." He is finishing up a college degree in medical technology. He is a nice guy.

Three years ago he met a lovely girl named Faye. They began to date. They became intimate. Their future looked rosy. "We got along quite well together and it seemed we had a lot in common," Monroe says. He did all the nice things that nice guys do. And she seemed to reciprocate: "She would call me at home and tell me how much she looked forward to our next meeting," Monroe says. "I was becoming seriously involved with her and I was very happy with that feeling." This went on for ten weeks.

And then the bottom dropped out. Monroe was invited to Faye's house for dinner. To say that Faye acted a little chilly is like saying Alaska is a little nippy in January. Monroe, being no fool, knew something was wrong. He asked her what was up. She explained that she had only been going out with him because she had recently broken up with her old boyfriend and she had been lonely. She needed, in her words, "someone to fill in." Since she and her boyfriend had now made up, she no longer needed Monroe. It was "Hit the road, Monroe" time.

What hurt, Monroe says, was not just that he, "a handsome, loving, and sensitive person with a bright future" was no longer needed or wanted, but that he was being replaced by "a tattoo artist who had hurt her both mentally and physically. A real loser."

Dump No. 2 happened while Monroe was working in the microbiology department of a hospital. His supervisor, an older divorced woman, invited him to her house one evening. And then "she seduced me," Monroe says. Again Monroe was a nice guy, doing the little things that nice guys do. The affair took off but after only a little while she called it off. When Monroe wanted to know why, she said it was simple. She had resumed her relationship with the drug addict she had met in a rehabilitation center.

Just a few months ago Monroe ran a personal ad stating that a "handsome, loving, and sensitive person with a bright future ahead of him" was

---

looking for "an unattached female." (When you think about it, it really doesn't sound like that much to ask for. Especially with the numbers being what they are, right?)

"I got a reply from a nice girl," says the nice guy. "She seemed like a real nice person and we started going out. After three months she called me and said, 'I'm pregnant.' It was a real shock. I said, 'Well, it's not my child.' She said no it wasn't, it was her old boyfriend's. She said they had broken up just before we started going out and she was going to quit school and marry him. He's nineteen and unemployed."

Monroe is now sure that it's not just love that's blind; it's women, too, who can't see the nice guys for the jerks. It's just not right that a terrific guy like him keeps getting thrown over for duds, losers, and clowns.

"I've asked a lot of people why women seem so attracted to losers but I've never gotten a straight answer," Monroe says.

He's not the only nice guy who, sadly, is starting to wonder if he needs to change his act. Jake's a commodities broker—also a nice guy—who can't figure women out. He has determined that the following rules hold true:

1. Women always want what they can't have.

2. When women get what they thought they wanted, they decide they don't want it anymore.

3. The nicer you are to a woman, the worse things become for you. The more you ignore them, the more they chase after you.

4. If a woman has no interest in you after dating for a period of time, all you have to do to renew her interest is pay attention to one of her friends in front of her.

That's been Sylvester's experience too. At first women seem to like him precisely because he *is* nice. He is gallant, the master of the grand gesture. He sends flowers, he opens doors. The women love it. Then they start hating it. They lose interest, some of them overnight. They *attack* him for the gestures, sneer at him when he reaches for the door. He wants to know if he is being "too nice." Is there such a thing as "too nice" in this world?

He has taken out women who want relationships to happen overnight. Women who end relationships overnight. He doesn't know how to act anymore, and he hates himself for monitoring what he says and does.

But he has decided that there must be a system for finding someone who wants a truly nice guy, that people are methodical about finding a car or a house and that he would be just as systematic about finding a woman who wants a nice guy. So Sylvester, a thirty-eight-year-old businessman, interviews women, often on the first date. He asks them how they feel about children. Whether they like nice, honest men. If they iron.

"I know it sounds like a strange way to do it, but if you're incompatible, what is the point of staying? Why start something that will be hurtful later on? When I was younger I was willing to take the time and do the flirting, and then go through the pain of losing someone, but now let's get that over with, please." And if a woman isn't going to like his ongoing niceness, Sylvester adds, he wishes she would indicate that early on, too.

Mr. Gotta Keep Moving On

This man is so afraid of commitment he wears his clothes loose. His theme song is "Baby, Baby Don't Get Hooked on Me." Oh, he can be a wonderful guy, all right, charming, the life of the party, and after he's gone, you can remember exactly what you loved about him. You just can't remember *him* very well. 'Cause when the relationship gets going, so does he.

Barry is a Mr. Gotta Keep Moving On although when Janice met him she didn't know it. She thought he was perfect. They were the same religion, both thirty-three, both professionals. He was an attorney, she a designer. Neither had ever been married.

Barry was bright, nice-looking. Janice felt like she could trust him 100 percent and not worry about whether he was lying or cheating. They had been fixed up by mutual friends and hit it off so well on their first date that the next day they both called the couple that had fixed them up to say thanks.

And after that first night they were off to the races. They would have dinner a couple of nights a week after work; they spent every weekend together. He brought her fresh flowers every week. He said, "I love you." He introduced her to his parents, his business contacts. He helped her start her own graphics business.

"He just fit what I had in mind," Janice says. And she thought that Barry felt the same way about her.

After about eleven months Janice started to think, "This is it. All the indications from what he said and did were that we would be making plans for the future. I thought we would get engaged in a few months and talk about getting married in the next year. When two people are in their thirties, exclusively seeing each other, involved with each other's families, what other conclusion is there to draw, right?"

Not exactly.

One sunny day Janice told Barry, "We should talk." She told him that she didn't need to get engaged right away but that she wanted to know what he was thinking. Barry said he was thinking about his business. He elaborated. He said, "I think you want more from this relationship than I do right now. This is the most difficult thing I have ever done, more difficult than preparing for a trial, but I can't give you what I think you want."

Janice pressed him. "I said, 'It's okay if we don't get married next week, but is there any future?' "

Barry said he wanted to feel free to see her or not see her and not feel as if he had to make plans with her. He wanted to go back to casual dating. Anyone who has ever tried this knows it's like paddling upstream, or trying to walk backward through a whole day, but Janice said she would try it. They would go back to him calling her up and asking her out for Saturday night. She would bite her tongue every time she started to say, "Let's do something Sunday afternoon," or "Let's get together after work." She tried it but it didn't work.

"I felt we had been too involved to casually date again," Janice says. "And I figured why keep investing my energy in a relationship that wasn't going to work out. He came over to get a project I had done for him and I finally said, 'This is it.' He picked up the project and said, 'Okay.' "

Now and then they bump into each other on the street and when they do they kiss hello and good-bye. But inside Janice feels angry. She wants to ask, "How dare you lead me on with everything you say and do and then all of a sudden tell me you want to take ten steps back?"

But she has a feeling that if she decided to tell him that, she'd have to shout it after his disappearing back. He'd be long gone before she got all the words out.

The Sucker

He's the excitement junkie who ends up high and dry, looking through his empty pockets. He's the guy who makes a beeline for the kind of woman guaranteed to leave him lonely. There are a lot of great women out there, but he's not interested. He only has eyes for the woman whose eyes are on her own mirror. He likes the highs and lows, the peaks and valleys—or the valleys and canyons when she starts treating him like dirt. Which she always does, sooner or later.

Ira's a Sucker. He's a traveling salesman and by his own description, a good-time guy. He says his job is to fly around the country and take people to lunch. He is forty-two, divorced for ten years. He has been through the "I hate all women" stage and the "I'm going to jump on every woman" stage. And when he saw Lisa, a waitress in a coffee shop near his office, he thought maybe he was finally in the "I'm ready to settle down" stage.

They started to date in September a few years ago. Ira would call her up and say, "How'd you like to go out tonight?" and Lisa would hem and haw: "I don't know . . . I really shouldn't . . . Maybe another time." So Ira would sweeten the pot: "Let's try that new fancy restaurant downtown." And Lisa would grab her coat.

Still, there was always a part of herself that she held back. "She was always very aloof," Ira says. "I told myself she needed to know me better, that she had been through some rough times emotionally and needed to get over them. I tried to talk to her about it, but she would always change the subject."

Christmas came and Ira gave Lisa a complete head-to-toe outfit to the tune of $300. Dress, shoes, the works. She gave him a bottle of Polo aftershave. "Not even cologne," Ira says. He took her on trips to Tampa, New York, and other hot spots. He always paid the bills. She said, "I've got to have you over to dinner sometime."

Sometime never came.

Ira excused all of it. "I figured this poor kid really had a hard time of it. I thought things would change. And I wanted this to be different than my other escapades."

Because Ira travels so much, restaurants are no big deal to him. So he thought that as a special treat he would prepare dinner one Saturday night for Lisa and two of his friends. He made spaghetti with homemade sauce that takes three hours to cook, and homemade noodles. He even made his own salad dressing. He stayed home all afternoon cooking. His friends arrived on time. Lisa didn't. He called her. She said something had come up and she had to work that night. When he called the restaurant later, they said she wasn't there.

It was a pretty quiet dinner party.

"My friends thought I was nuts to put up with her," Ira says. "But I still believed there was good in her, underneath all the other stuff."

He called her a few days after the no-show and she said she *had* worked that night but at a *different* restaurant. Right.

"I knew she was lying to me," he says. "But my self-esteem wouldn't let me see it for what it was. I don't think anyone likes rejection."

Through business connections Ira can get great seats to concerts. Lisa was dying to see Prince that year, so Ira got two tickets for her and her girlfriend. Then Dolly Parton was scheduled to appear and Lisa asked for six tickets.

"It was one of the few times she ever called me," Ira says. "I just assumed we would go along with four of her friends. I wound up getting ninth-row tickets. I gave her four tickets and she said, 'Where are the other two?' I said, 'I thought they were for you and me.' She said no, they were *all* for her friends. I was ticked off, but I gave them to her."

Ira had an idea—who wouldn't?—that Lisa just might be at that concert. He called her that night and, sure enough, she wasn't at home. He got his proof from friends of his who found themselves sitting down the aisle from her. They said that not only was she there, she was there with another man. That's when the pieces finally fell together. But it took Ira another few months to remove the "Kick Me" sign from the seat of his pants.

"It was an education," Ira says. "People pay for their educations, and I sure paid for mine."

He doesn't think he has much to be grateful for when it comes to his relationship with Lisa—other than it's over—but he would feel very grateful if he compared notes with George, whose tab ran a whole lot higher.

George is a thirty-year-old man who works in the family business and spends a lot of time at bars. He was at one of his favorite spots when he got the eye from Gretchen, who at the time was wearing black stirrup pants and very high heels.

"She came over and we started talking and she starts to tell me all kinds of things about myself: what kind of leather jacket I wear in the winter, who my friends are. I'm a little shocked. I say, 'How do you know?' She says she has been watching me for a year and a half."

Who wouldn't be intrigued? Who wouldn't be flattered? George certainly was and they began dating. They went out three or four times a week: the beach, dinner, concerts, movies. "For a month it was great," George says. "Then things started to get a little funny."

Gretchen is twenty-seven; she has been divorced for two years. She told George she rarely dated a guy more than once. He found this flattering but a little scary too. She also started telling him stories about her old boyfriends. "This guy was an idiot, that one was a jerk." This always sets off alarms in a man: he wonders whether he'll be the idiot in the next story.

They were at a bar one night when things came to a head. They were both in lousy moods, and when George noted how pretty another woman was, Gretchen blew up. She stalked off to the ladies' room and half an hour later appeared on the dance floor with another man. But it was after she threw her drink in George's face that they decided to call it quits.

George missed her a little, but what he really missed, he freely admits, was "not having her on my arm. She was great to be seen around with."

Over the next few months they bumped into each other, and in November she called him. She said she wanted to go out again. By December things were going so well that he suggested they go to Las Vegas together for New Year's Eve. He plunked down $1,100 for airplane tickets and a hotel room and volunteered to pay for everything else—meals, shows, etc. He even bought her a weekend wardrobe including a black strapless dress to wear on New Year's Eve. They were supposed to leave December 28.

On December 27 George called Gretchen and said, "I'm staying home tonight to pack; I hope you are too."

Gretchen said that actually, she was going out with some friends.

"I was supposed to pick her up at eight in the morning so it made me a little nervous to hear she was going out," George says. And with good reason. At 3:30 A.M.—six hours before they were supposed to be up, up and away—the telephone rang. It was Gretchen.

She said, "I'm not going."

George said, "Are you at home?"

She said no.

He said, "Are you with your girlfriends?"

She said no.

George decided to go to Las Vegas alone. He didn't want to lose all his money, of course, but the real reason he went was that he was afraid that if he stayed in town he would have run into Gretchen. And he knew she would have been with another man, and wearing the dress that George had bought her.

There's no sure-fire way to know which of the men and which of the women are going to find each other, and whether their romances will work or whether they won't. It might be Ms. Rumpelstiltskin and Mr. Gotta Keep Moving On. Trouble. Or Ms. Picky-Picky-Picky and Mr. Nice Guy. More trouble. But all kinds of unusual pairs fall in love for all kinds of reasons. Keep reading to find out why people make the choices they do, against all odds, every single day.

4

Chemistry 101:
What Makes People
Fall in Love?

What makes people fall in love? Is it (1) cold, hard cash? (2) charisma? (3) concern about being buried next to their parents? (4) commitment to the species' survival? (5) All the above?

Or is it *chemistry?*

Chemistry is all about how love is supposed to hit you. Some people say it doesn't exist. Well, it does, but it takes a lot of different forms. Sometimes you mix two chemicals and get a slow burn; other times an explosion. For some folks chemistry works like the Asian flu: one minute you're walking around and the next thing you know you're knocked off your feet. Others take a long time to admit that what snuck up on them so gently is in fact that very thing called love.

It Took Her *About a Minute*

Didi is a disciple of the quick swoon. She knew she was in love after an hour. The only problem was that she had to convince Brad that he felt the same way. That took a little longer.

"I was busy," he explains.

Brad and Didi, both twenty-one, met in a night class at a local college.

"I noticed her, I liked her," he says. On the last day of class he invited her to a baseball game.

"After the date he took me to Clyde's Donuts, where he had a week-end job," Didi says. "He gave me a dozen to take home." By this time she was over the edge; perfectly matched diamonds couldn't have made her any happier. After their good-night kiss she walked into her house, closed the door, and leaned against it for a good ten minutes, "the donuts held close to my heart."

This had all begun as one of those cases where he and she go out on a first date and have a wonderful time. *She* knows it. He walks her to her front door, looks lovingly into her eyes, and says, "I'll call you soon." He *means* it. But then he falls off the face of the earth for five weeks.

One day went by. Two. Three. No Brad. A week. Two weeks. "All I did was complain, cry, and act miserable," says the lovestruck Didi. "My parents avoided me, my friends tried to console me. Everybody said to forget about him, but I couldn't."

Brad has another explanation.

"What happened was, I was just starting a career in data processing and I spent most of my time working. I was busy."

Three weeks went by. Four weeks. Five.

Didi was not idle during this time. She would cruise Brad's neighborhood several times a week. "Just to be near him." She was pretty far gone.

"I had no idea she was driving by," Brad says. "I remember being outside working on my car, but I never saw her."

Didi decided to take more drastic measures. She left work early one day, stopped at a liquor store, bought a couple of piña colada "Cocktails for Two" and a few magazines, and drove to the campus. She thought Brad was taking a computer class that night and she decided to "bump into him." She found his car in the parking lot, settled in with her magazines and liquid courage, and waited. And waited. For five hours.

"I finally left a note on his windshield," she says. " 'Hi Brad! I was here at school studying (Ha!) and I saw your car, so I thought I'd say hi. Call me sometime, okay? I'm leaving for vacation in Aruba in three days. Didi.' "

Then she drove home and parked herself by the telephone.

Actually, Brad had sold his car to his brother and when his brother got home from school that night the first thing he said was "Who's Didi?"

Now you might think at this point that Brad would rush right over to his telephone and call Didi, who by this time had already been fully in love for five weeks. But *nooooooo*. Brad did not.

"I was very busy," he says.

Two days later he actually did pick up the phone. "I knew she was leaving. I figured I had better call."

Just in the nick of time, it turns out.

"I clearly remember sitting on my girlfriend's bed—we were leaving the next morning—and being more miserable than I had ever been in my life," Didi says. "Then the phone rang. It was my mom. She said, 'Brad just called. He says you should give him a call when you get back from vacation.' "

Well, Didi floated off to Aruba. And the only trip that has ever been better was her honeymoon with Brad in the Bahamas in 1983.

"I would have called at some time, even if she didn't leave the note," Brad says. "But I'm glad she did. Feelings aren't always equal. Some people grow into their feelings. Others feel them immediately."

She Stopped Traffic

You think Didi knew fast? Meet Amanda. She had an idea that Phil might be that special someone, or at least *a* special someone, after a once-over that took about three seconds, give or take. And she risked total, public humiliation to check out her hunch.

When it happened, she happened to look her worst. Isn't it always that way? She had just gone jogging. She was sweaty and her hair was a mess. She had finished her run, jumped in her car, and was on her way in the door of a convenience store for a muffin and coffee. Phil was on his way out. He was wearing overalls and carrying two ice cream cones. He had just delivered a load of beer next door. He was gorgeous.

On his way to his truck he said hi to Amanda. That was it. One little "hi." Then he climbed into his semi-trailer and handed his partner one of the ice cream cones. Amanda kept walking into the store.

"He had these blue eyes, and I looked into his face and thought to myself, 'Here you go again. You see someone you think is attractive and that's the end of it.' "

She bought herself a muffin, walked out, and looked around, but the hunk in the overalls, his partner, and their truck were all gone. Amanda cursed her luck and climbed into her car.

But her luck was better than she thought. Ten minutes later, she found herself stuck in traffic. She glanced over and realized with a jolt that she was inching along near the very same beer truck that the gorgeous man in the parking lot had climbed into. She waved up at him as her car overtook his, and he waved back. Then the truck pulled ahead.

Finally traffic came to a complete standstill. Amanda put her car in Park in the center lane of the busy highway. She jumped out and ran up to the truck.

"Phil looked over at me," she says. "The whole encounter lasted about ten seconds."

This is what the encounter consisted of: She asked him if he was single. He nodded yes. She said if he ever wanted to buy her an ice cream cone, here was her number. He nodded again. And she shoved her card up at him and through his window.

"He never really opened his mouth during the whole thing," she says.

Luck always plays a heavy hand in this kind of story. In this case, it not only landed Amanda and Phil in the same traffic jam, but landed Phil on the passenger side on this particular day. It turns out that he usually drives the truck. If he had been, Amanda never would have seen him, since the truck was on her left in the traffic tie-up.

Following her brazen act Amanda jumped back in her car, praying for the light to turn green and for traffic to open up so she could get out of there. And she was so nervous that she suddenly had a sinking feeling that she had shoved her supervisor's card, which she had in her purse, through the truck window by mistake.

She hadn't. Phil called four days later and asked her out. They went to the races on their first date. It was the best first date either of them can remember. And Amanda is grateful that she followed her impulse and performed the single most gutsy act of her life.

Neither One's a 10 but Their Love Is

Love at first sight doesn't necessarily mean you love what you see. Herb and Charlene fell in love almost instantly, but they both admit that quick as their love affair took off, it would have been stalled at ground zero if it had been determined by what met their eyes.

They are both part-time theater ushers. Charlene is thirty-eight and overweight. Herb is fifty and balding. One night they found themselves working the same aisle of the theater. In between seating people they started to chat about a show they had both recently seen. Herb was impressed with Charlene's "wit, knowledge, and intellectual curiosity." Charlene was fascinated by Herb's "intelligence, enthusiasm, and sense of fun." (Notice that neither of them said anything about the other's shape, size, or eye color.) Charlene left the theater feeling "oddly exhilarated but didn't stop to pinpoint the cause."

Herb followed up their brief encounter with a complimentary note asking Charlene for a date.

"At the end of that first date, I was halfway convinced she was the end of a twenty-five-year search," Herb says. "Within a week, I was fully convinced."

"Before I could recover from the shock of having an actual *date,* we were making wedding plans," Charlene says. "We are so in love and so grateful to fate and our good sense. I like to say that we fell in love from the inside out, the way a lasting relationship must."

Now that they're happily married, Herb and Charlene can look back honestly and assess their first impressions. When Charlene first saw Herb, she indeed noticed that not only was he ten years older and balding, but "worst of all he was wearing a suit and tie which I always associate with the words 'stuffy' and 'boring.' "

And Herb adds, "My wife and I freely admit that if we had been at a party, neither of us would have been attracted enough by the other's outward appearance to go over and start a conversation. It's almost scary that if this had been the case, we would have missed the meeting that has changed and enriched both our lives. But I had first become acquainted with her inner self and was so delighted with that that I found that I didn't care what was on the outside. I grew to love the whole outer person, imperfections and all."

To Herb and Charlene, being in love with someone short of a 10 has its definite advantages:

"We don't have to worry about our greatest assets becoming gray or wrinkled," Herb says.

Charlene adds, "Tell the authors of those personal ads to quit looking for the perfect face and figure and open up to life's fabulous possibilities."

Cold, Hard Chemistry

While some love affairs begin with moonlit walks, Mallory and Ted's came to life over a checkbook.

They were both teachers and pretty good friends—nothing more. Ted had made it a rule never to date anyone he worked with. Mallory understood. But when she left teaching to go into real estate she sent him a note, just to keep in touch. The note came at a time when Ted was kind of low. His best buddy had just moved out of town and it had left a void in his life. He needed someone to pal around, have dinner, go to the movies with. Mallory was available.

"Neither of us was seeing anybody and we both wanted to go places so we just started going together," Ted says nonchalantly. "We'd make sure that the other wasn't going to be alone on a Saturday night. We would spend it together; I'd cook a nice meal, sometimes we would just watch TV. We liked each other a lot and eventually we became each other's best friend. But I never thought of marrying her."

Meanwhile, both Ted and Mallory were each living in one-bedroom apartments.

"I wanted a house for myself," Ted says. "I was tired of paying rent and I wanted the tax deduction. But all I could afford on my income were real fix-ups or decent places in bad neighborhoods. Mallory said she wanted a house too. One night after quite a few Southern Comforts I said, 'Gee, with both our incomes put together we could afford something nice.' I said, 'If you can find a house we both like, why don't we get married?'"

Not the most romantic wedding proposal.

"She was shocked. She never expected a great passionate love in her life. In fact, she truly believed no one would ever ask her to marry him. She has an aunt who never married and she always said she would end up like her. I had had romances and they always hurt too much in the end or else I had seen my great burning passion die out," Ted says. "I really wasn't in the market.

"Well, I don't know if she quite believed me or what, but she said she would look around for a house. The next day I left town to visit my brother. When I got back a week later, she picked me up at the airport and told me she had found a house. She had found it the day I left. Then I started to get cold feet. I thought, what am I getting into—a house, a wife—so I made a really low offer."

The owners accepted it.

Ted and Mallory got married. Their first year was spent getting used to each other. "We did fine. We were both getting what we wanted. We had the house, a dual income. We were able to get a nicer car and buy some nice things for ourselves."

But something funny happened to Ted and Mallory. Somewhere in the second or third year of their marriage they fell in love.

"I don't know exactly when it happened," Ted says. "But it did. We went from being best friends to being in love. Now I can't imagine not having her around. Sometimes we sit around—I still cook a great meal on Saturday nights—and we have a bottle of wine and talk about how it took a house to bring us together. Neither of us can believe we've been married for nine years."

A Second Chance Saved It

In this fast-food, fast-times, fast-paced world where one chance is all anyone usually gets, what makes some people hang in there and give someone a second shot?

Harry isn't sure. But he's one of those people who gave the chemical reaction time to seep into his system and take hold slowly. He had worked down the hall from Cecilia for three long years. He felt no huge rush of hormones when he passed her in the hall. His heart never went flip-flop at the sight of her disappearing into her office. But one day when she admired the Renoir print on his desk, he decided to ask her to lunch. It was no big deal.

The meal was a disaster on both sides. Cecilia wasn't exactly swept away by Harry's idea of a lunch date, traipsing through the company's cafeteria line together. Harry was totally turned off. Cecilia was wearing a "horrible outfit," she wouldn't look him in the eye, and worst of all, it seemed from the way she talked that she spent all her free time in an active search for available men. "I thought that was pretty shallow," Harry says.

He walked her back down the hall after lunch, said a feeble good-bye, and that was it. He labeled her a BUP. That's his acronym for "Boring, Uptight, and Prudish." Three qualities guaranteed to remove her as a candidate for anything in his life other than a one-shot lunch date. He was sure this was one woman he would never be seeing again. Except for maybe in the hall.

About a month later they ran into each other—in the hall. Harry had no real desire to strike up a conversation. When Cecilia asked him what he had been up to lately, he just said, "Riding my bike."

Cecilia said, "Oh, I ride my bike too!" He said well, maybe they would go biking together sometime. But it was Cecilia who called Harry a couple of days later and asked him. For some reason he said okay, though he had been planning on staying home that day. And off they went. Harry thinks now that he was impressed that she took the initiative to call him. Not that he was excited about the outing but she went out on a limb, so what the heck.

"We had a pretty good time," he says. Good enough for him to ask her to an art fair. And that was good enough for him to invite her over to watch a TV special a few days later.

And slowly the BUP impression started to fade. First went the uptight and prudish part. He learned that she had been involved for ten years with a man twenty years her senior. This made him rethink the way he had her pegged. "I suddenly realized there is a lot to find out about this person and I don't really know anything about her," he says. Then out went the boring part. The fact was that he had a good time with her. They had a lot in common. They had a lot to talk about.

After about a month Harry stopped seeing the other woman he was involved with.

Since then he has spent a lot of time trying to look back and pinpoint the exact moment when he decided to start seeing Cecilia exclusively. He also tried to determine what it was that made him give her a second chance. It may have been nothing more than the fact that he had nothing to do on a Saturday afternoon. Or that he admired a woman like Cecilia who took a chance. "Calling me was something a boring, uptight, prudish woman would never do," he says. He can't quite pin down all the reasons that he hung in there.

But he did—and now after nine months of dating they're moving in together.

Diamonds in the Rough

As Harry knows, it's no great trick to pick out a big shiny diamond while it's all sparkling and staring you in the face. But it's harder to nurture the diamond while it's still in the rough. Like Harry, Barbara gave her great find some time, and now she's the lucky one.

Two weeks after she moved out on her husband, living alone for the first time in her life, she knocked on the next door apartment. She needed a screwdriver to hang a wall lamp and she knew the place belonged to two men. She had met one of them before. This time the other one answered.

He looked as if he was about seventeen. He was raw, not at all sophisticated. He was not terribly appealing. Barbara looked at him and wondered, "Why isn't he in high school?" It turned out that Jerry was twenty-three and a salesman, and sophisticated or not, raw or not, he did help her put up her new lamp. She found him quiet and laid-back and not at all the salesman type.

A week later he asked Barbara out to a movie and when she invited him inside for dessert he leaned over to kiss her. That made her nervous. It had been eight years since she had been out on a date. Sure she was lonely but she was afraid of getting involved too quickly just to ease that empty feeling. She took a deep breath and said, "I guess I should explain to you how I feel."

Jerry said she didn't have to. He understood.

And with those few words he worked his way into her heart.

"It only takes one major thing for me to make up my mind about someone and in this case he was so sensitive, so considerate," Barbara says. And most surprising of all, so mature.

But still, he looked so young and so raw. Sometimes Barbara was self-conscious about it when they went out. But she didn't let it get to her enough to make her brush him off. Nor did she listen to her friends, who told her she was crazy to get so involved with the very first man she met after her separation.

Her feelings grew. "I began to realize that women should look for in a man what it is that attracts them to a girlfriend and makes that friendship last. Naturally there has to be attraction, too, but more important is the friendship and the comfortable, easy feeling you get from someone that you like."

About a year after they met, Barbara and Jerry were married. That was eleven years and two kids ago. And you'll be happy to know that Jerry has filled out, grown up, and really turned into something of a hunk. He's funny and kind of cool.

And after eleven years Barbara still runs to the door when she hears his key in the lock. She says it sounds a little corny, but "I just feel good all over when I see him. My heart still skips a beat when he comes home, and at the movies we still hold hands. Even when he goes on the road with women ten years my junior, I still don't worry.

"They wouldn't have been lined up behind either of us in the singles bars, where judgments are made in seconds," she adds. "But we took time to look deeper despite our doubts and it paid off."

Magnetic Attraction

Chemistry brings people together and it also keeps them together. Sometimes in ways and for reasons only they can fathom. It operates according to its own rules, or no rules. And in the end it's not meant to be understood, only appreciated.

Todd was thirty-four when he met Frannie in a bar, and kind of a drifter. She was twenty-six and pretty much the same type. She had a four-year-old daughter but no husband. Just a good-for-nothing ex-boyfriend. She was unemployed, living off her daughter's Aid to Dependent Children checks. Frannie and Todd started hanging around together.

A month after they met, she moved into his place. She was having trouble making her rent payments and had nowhere else to go.

"I knew things were going too fast, I knew we weren't doing them in the proper order," Todd says. But even so, things were pretty good at first and he liked having her around. He even thought maybe they would get married one of these days. But after a month or two Frannie started to withdraw.

"She got real quiet," Todd says. "She would go out on the back porch by herself and read all the time like she had a lot on her mind. I felt bad for her at first."

And then Todd found out that Frannie was seeing her ex-boyfriend again. "She was living with me and seeing someone else. I told her to leave."

She did. That was seven years ago. They said good-bye but they have never really been able to break it off. Every six or seven weeks Todd gets a call from Frannie. They're all pretty much the same thing.

"She'll say, 'How've you been? What are you doing?' She'll mention something about her apartment building or her mom or her sister. Within a couple of minutes she'll say, 'Well, do you feel like taking a ride out to see me?' She lives fifty miles away. I say, 'I guess so.' That's about as sentimental as it gets."

Then Todd drives out to see her and stays with her a couple of days. They'll have a few drinks, go out to dinner, maybe see a movie or go for a walk. Over Halloween they took her daughter—she's eleven now—to see a haunted house. They talk and make love.

"Then things don't work so well and I just leave," Todd says. "It just seems to happen. I don't know if she thinks it's what I want or I think it's what she wants. It just happens. I'll just say, 'Okay, I'll see ya,' and I'll be gone."

And that's it.

"It's not a big romantic deal," Todd says. "But I guess in a way it is. These are still the best and most romantic dates of my life. . . . Do I love her? I don't know what love is. But I know she is always close in my mind. I look out for her and try to help her. I get along with her for some reason. There are no underlying methods or tactics to what she's doing. I've gone with a few girls, although I haven't had much experience, and I've found most of them have some kind of subplot to what they're doing. This girl doesn't.

"It's been going on so long between us, it will probably go on forever. When she doesn't call for a real long time I'm a little aggravated. But I never call her. When I hear her voice I just think, well, it's Frannie again. I'm happy in a way, but that's because there's nothing else in my life. I know she's had a couple of boyfriends in between but I guess nothing works out too well for her either. Still, I know we could never make it any more permanent. When she's drinking, she'll talk about us maybe getting married but I tell her, 'Who are you kidding?' "

Explain that one if you can. You can't. Chemistry works in strange and mysterious ways.

5

Social Diseases

The symptoms for these social diseases are hard to spot at first; there's no fever, no chills. But there may be that sinking feeling in the pit of your stomach that something is terribly wrong with your love life. You keep falling for the same losers. You give up the good folks for the jerks. Or maybe you've retired from dating altogether. You just can't get your life together. (Your love life, that is. You're probably going gangbusters at work.) Put your symptoms next to the following diseases and see if you're suffering from any of these modern maladies.

The "Let's Make a Deal" Syndrome

Do you trade "up" in the dating game? Are you ready to give up that sure Saturday night date for an unknown quantity hidden behind Door No. 3? And when you look back at your dating record, have you sometimes given up a catch for a loser?

Irene, single and thirty-three, recently realized that she has been playing "Let's Make a Deal" for nearly fifteen years.

She could have been married by now. But she always figured there would be someone better—some yet unknown, completely perfect guy—just around the corner. Someone really terrific, a combination of Bruce Willis and Dan Rather, behind Door No. 2, or behind the curtain, or in the bigger box on the showroom floor. So Irene never held on to what she had:

"It's just exactly like on 'Let's Make a Deal,'" she explains. "I grew up with that show and it's the best analogy I can use to describe my pattern. I've had some wonderful men in my life. But it's as if Monty Hall had chosen me from all the screaming people and given me a little box. In it, let's say, there'd be a perfectly gorgeous emerald ring and I love it. But when he offers me the chance to throw it all away for the unknown thing behind the curtain, I do it. Who knows? I always figure the next boyfriend might be that much more perfect, just like there might be a cruise and a car behind the curtain."

Or there might be a donkey and a bale of hay.

Irene had a boyfriend in college named Roger. He was smart and sweet and they dated for three years. They even taught Sunday school together while they were students. After school he went off to study law and he wanted her to come with him. She said no.

Why?

She could easily tick off the reasons: She was only twenty-one, the world was at her feet, she didn't want to live in New York, Roger wasn't really perfect.

Those were the obvious reasons. But there was another one. Deep down, she believed that whoever was hiding behind the next door or the next curtain would be better. Whoever would come along at the next job or in the next city she lived in. Whoever she might happen to bump into at the grocery store or be introduced to during the next fix-up. He'd be smarter, more handsome, sexier, more ambitious, more compatible. Just better. She was sure of it. So, after three years of steady, totally committed dating, she gave Roger the brush-off.

Just like that.

She went instead for Door No. 1, which is where she found Walter. It wasn't a terrible trade, all things considered. Walter was never going to be as successful as Roger, but he was also nice and he seemed to fit in with that period of Irene's life. They were both in the advertising business, both athletic. It was a good relationship. Walter wanted to make it a permanent one. For two years he asked her to marry him, for two years she said no. Finally, he said good-bye.

But Irene still wasn't worried. Walter hadn't seemed quite right. She loved him but she didn't know if she would love him in ten years. Also, there were things she liked in Roger that Walter didn't have. The next trade would be better, she was sure. A combination of the best of Roger and the best of Walter.

Well, since Walter, Irene has made a series of trades. She has given up each of the men she has dated, sure that she would be trading up. But most of the trades have been lateral. Like trading a gas range for a sofa bed—no clear outcome. And there are times she'd like to kick herself. She has done the dating equivalent of trading away the two-week all-expenses-paid vacation in Jamaica for a travel alarm clock.

She has always assumed that the succession of boyfriends would be like a steady climb up a ladder, a series of better, and finally best, trades. But when she's really honest with herself, she has to admit that no one has ever made her feel as special as Roger, boyfriend No. 1. No relationship has lasted as long as that one did, either. And now there are times when Irene wishes that way back when she was twenty-one she had kept the little box and not gone crazy for the curtain.

"In my head at the time there was a little voice telling me to look for someone new," she says. "It was like all those voices on the game show screaming 'Trade! Trade! Take the curtain!' I'm sure a lot of the contestants on the show went home wishing they hadn't listened to those voices and their own greed. Sometimes I wish I hadn't listened to my own voice way back then. I know I'm going to meet someone. But I've stopped thinking there will be a huge qualitative leap from one boyfriend to the next."

The Carton Complex

Do you trip over boxes of books and pots and pans? Do you put off painting your apartment, hanging shelves, giving parties? Are you waiting until your *real* life starts—once you're married—to get on with living?

Donna lives in the Old Town neighborhood of Chicago in a cute little apartment. The wallpaper in the kitchen is not exactly what she would have chosen for herself—it's a series of little bunnies nibbling littler carrots—but that's about the worst thing you can say about the place. And when the landlord increased the rent this year, it wasn't by much, so Donna happily signed a new lease.

She has been there, all told, for four years. And there's no reason to believe she'll be moving out soon. No job transfer looming. No windfall on the way for a down payment on a condo. But despite the fact that Donna's immediate future seems to be right there in that Old Town one-bedroom, the corner of the dining room is piled with boxes. There are about five of them. Cartons filled with books, with Pyrex, with things she doesn't need right away but figures she will someday when the real chapter of her life gets under way.

Donna, twenty-nine, suffers from the Carton Complex. She won't come right out and say it, but Donna believes that sooner or later a man will enter her life and whisk her away. They will set up a home together. That will be her *real* home. He will hang her pictures. She will use the Pyrex to fix them meals. They will read the books together. Right now, she's in transition. So she doesn't unpack the books or hang the pictures. She leaves them in the cartons in the corner.

"It's not just the cartons in the dining room," Donna admits. "In other little ways I put off acknowledging that I am a single person living on my own and completely responsible for taking care of myself and, furthermore, that this may be the situation for some time to come. Or maybe forever. Here's an example: I really should put up hooks on the back of the bathroom door to hold my towels. But I keep putting it off. I find myself thinking, 'I'm not going to be here that much longer. I'll probably be moving.' And when I ask myself, 'Why do you say that?' the reason I come up with is that someone is going to come into my life and take care of me or take me away from here altogether. Then he'll put up the hooks and we'll hang our 'His and Hers' towels from them. And then we'll unpack the boxes together and keep the empty ones in our garage."

Don't get the wrong idea about Donna. She's not some poor little helpless thing who can't change a light bulb. Not at all. She actually does quite well by herself. She has a tool box and knows more than a little about automotive repairs. She is familiar with the basics of plumbing and has put in her own telephone jack. She selected a long-distance carrier based on their relative attributes and knows what the tax bill means for her. She has lived on her own for seven years. It's not that she is waiting for a handyman to hang the bathroom hooks. That's not it. She's waiting for the man to make the hooks worthwhile. Then, and only then, will she get on with what she considers her real life.

You've seen this woman before. She's the one who swears her real life will begin when she loses ten pounds. *Then* she'll buy new clothes, get her hair done, go away on a great vacation that will be the start of a whole new existence. Just as soon as those ten pounds come off. And she'll start tomorrow. Donna is a variation on that theme.

"It's embarrassing to talk about because it makes me out to be a total jerk, the kind of woman who says, 'My life is nothing without a man' and I'm not that way. I am a very busy and generally a very happy person.

But I really have resisted setting up a real home for myself. So something obviously is going on."

No matter how rational Donna sounds about it, the cartons remain in the dining room. Neatly packed and piled. Taking up space. One of these days, Donna has decided, she is going to dig in and unpack them. She says she'll make room for the books; she'll put away the Pyrex cookware and throw the cardboard boxes into the garbage. She figures that will be the day life plays a neat little ironic trick and she ends up meeting the man of her dreams. Isn't that the way it always works?

Women aren't the only ones to suffer from the Carton Complex. Jim has it, too. "Why do you think I postpone buying nice dishes and eat off this set my mother gave me? Do you think I have a nice set of silver, although I could well afford it? Do you think I put my heart into choosing furniture? I'm waiting, too. The only difference between me and Donna is that my cartons are in my garage."

The "I Quit" Syndrome

Have you stopped accepting fix-ups and blind dates? Have you ceased checking out every gathering for unattached members of the opposite sex? Have you called a halt to instinctively staring at ring fingers on left hands? Have you stopped dating, period? You're not alone.

Judy, thirty-seven, had been dating pretty much nonstop since she was thirteen. "That's twenty-four years I've put in so far," she says. "I realized I must be doing something wrong."

In Judy's opinion, dating was not supposed to be an end in itself. It was supposed to lead to something. It was supposed to lead to marriage.

When it didn't, she felt like a violinist who's been rehearsing for twenty-four years and has never had a performance. It was as if she had taken twenty-four years of piano lessons and never given a single concert. So she decided to call a halt.

"This summer I decided I had had enough disappointments. I don't want to play this dating game anymore."

So what has Judy done? She slipped a little gold band around her third finger, left hand.

"I've taken myself out of the race. I needed a break. I'm taking the summer off. I just needed a couple of months to get myself together. I don't want to meet any new men, so I tell people I'm married. My friends used to fix me up with everybody. I told them to stop. I see my girlfriends and now I don't worry anymore; I don't have to race home to check on my answering machine."

It's not just women who have called it quits. John has also blown the whistle. After fifteen years of unhappy relationships, he figured if he needed this much pain he could just drop bowling balls on his foot.

John worked his way through college. He got by without student loans, scholarships, or rich parents. His true love, Nora, was not impressed. She wanted a little of the collegiate high life: concerts, movies, the nicer restaurants on Sunday nights, the little off-beat "I was just thinking of you, so I picked this up" gifts. John couldn't afford them. Nora told him he couldn't afford her.

"I was hurt by her attitude, but not crushed," says John.

For his next college girlfriend, he chose someone "more down to earth." Terra firma didn't move with Nancy, but "things seemed nice."

She was honest with him. She told him she didn't want any kind of exclusive commitment. She wanted to date around.

"I could accept that and had no problem with it until I learned that I was her last choice on a Friday night. She said I was better than sitting in the dorm." That wasn't quite the way John liked to think of himself so they parted company.

Then he got drafted just as Vietnam was winding down. He was seeing two girls, Meredith and Bonnie, at the time. Meredith's response to John's marching off to do his patriotic duty was to call him a "cold-hearted warmonger."

"I never could figure that one out," he says, shrugging.

Bonnie, on the other hand, promised to wait for him. But while he was gone, he got a "Dear John" letter. Not from Bonnie, but from her father. Dad said he felt badly for poor John because his daughter was not waiting around as she had pledged, she was sleeping around. John couldn't believe it. He didn't want to. So on his first leave, he traveled thousands of miles to see for himself what was going on.

"I thought her father was just trying to split us up," he says.

Unfortunately, he wasn't. Bonnie told John to "get lost" because she needed someone who was going to be reliable about showing her a good time.

After the Army, John went back to school and got his degree and then met Alicia, a girl who "made all the other bad experiences fade to insignificance." He and Alicia dated for two years and then became engaged. They set a date. But within months of the wedding, she got cold feet and decided she needed to see other men to test how she really felt about him.

She also decided to keep the one-and-a-half carat diamond engagement ring he had given her while she thought things over.

She left it to John to contact the guests, the church, the reception hall, and the caterer, to tell them that the wedding was off. When he came over one night to see if there was anything left of their relationship to salvage—like maybe the ring—her new boyfriend, who was an off-duty policeman, threatened to have John arrested for trespassing and a few other things.

Well, that was five years ago and John has had nothing to do with women since. He prefers the quiet, dull pain of loneliness to the active, throbbing pain of heartbreak, and he really doesn't believe romance can offer much in between. Sure he'd like to settle down with a nice woman. He'd also like to win the lottery. He puts his odds at both to be about the same. So for now, he's a dating dropout.

The New Celibacy

Vanessa has a very special anniversary coming. She's going to note the day—"celebrate" may be too strong a word—at an expensive French restaurant with a small group of friends. They'll have champagne, caviar, smoked salmon—all those overpriced foods associated with special occasions. And for dessert, chocolate torte.

"In the absence of sex, I think chocolate's the next best thing," says Vanessa.

Vanessa will be marking one year of celibacy: 365 days without sex. That's 52 Saturday nights, 52 Sunday mornings, one New Year's Eve, one Christmas, one birthday, one Fourth of July, all without fireworks.

One long, lonely year. It's the longest stretch of doing without she's had since she was eighteen.

She didn't set out to be celibate for a whole year. She was not trying for a place in the *Guinness Book of World Records.* It just crept up on this twenty-nine-year-old technical writer. In fact, she admits to being "a little floored by the whole thing."

She dated her last real boyfriend, a computer programmer, for four years. "Four years of complete futility," she says. "Four years of fighting and reconciling. There was a total lack of communication. We were completely different. Working at the same place was one of the few things we had in common. I finally said that anything is better than this. Being dateless is better than being with him."

Little did she know.

That was just over a year ago. Between the computer programmer and her one-year anniversary, Vanessa had a few scattered dates and one "brief and torrid affair."

And then she arrived at an important point in her life.

"Once the affair was over, I reached a point where I realized that it's just not fun to have sex for its own sake anymore. Something beyond the act has to make it worthwhile. Now I'm looking for fulfillment, communication, intimacy. Meaningful interaction. Without those things, sex just isn't satisfying anymore. And it's not that I'm afraid of AIDS or herpes. Maybe that's foolish on my part, but I haven't gotten close enough to anyone to worry about them. There just hasn't been anyone that I wanted to go home with."

The really interesting part of this story is that in these days when people talk openly about "safe sex," but less often about "no sex," Vanessa is not alone in her decision. Not by a long shot. Several of her girlfriends have also settled into celibacy. The AIDS epidemic has done it for some of them. Others are just tired of recreational sex.

Vanessa says there are good and bad parts to her new state. The good part: "It sure beats a lot of meaningless interludes, waking up and thinking, 'What did I do that for?' Feeling really empty. It gives me time to work on myself so when someone comes along, a real relationship becomes a possibility."

The bad part?

"You build up some fears. You start to wonder how attractive and desirable you are. But that just underscores how important I think it is to wait until you're with someone you trust and really care about."

In the meantime, Vanessa has not lost her sense of humor. She says she's toying with a new idea: a convent. "As long as I'm living the lifestyle, I might as well get the credit."

The Déjà Vu Dilemma

Have you been "in love" more times than you've been to Europe? Have you seriously considered marrying more people than you can count on your fingers? Does each new romance compete with the history of your past romances? Do you get that weird, hazy feeling that you've wandered down this road before? You're caught in the Déjà Vu Dilemma.

Frank Sinatra used to close his eyes and sing, "Love is lovelier/The second time around." But that was several decades ago, and even Frankie couldn't have predicted the times we're in now when people fall in love five or ten times—or more—before finally settling down. All this loving takes its toll.

Jody is twenty-nine, funny, charming, and sensitive. She has dated a string of rich, handsome men. They have taken her to picturesque Portuguese fishing villages, sleepy little Caribbean islands, and major European capitals. They have bought her a fur coat, assorted jewelry, innumerable meals as well as clothes, books, records, sporting equipment, posters, and pets. They have sworn they loved her. But not one wanted to marry her. And how does she feel? Miserable.

"Falling in love is so hard when you're in your late twenties, early thirties," Jody says. "You start to analyze it all. When you've been in love a few times, you start thinking of yourself as a used car. I started seeing a new man and I called him 'honey.' It was too soon and I saw him cringe when I did it. It made me feel so cheap. I think I still have a little innocence left in me, and I don't want to get cynical; I want to throw caution to the wind. Then there's that little voice in my head saying, 'Even if you buy him that gift, if you send him that card, if you write him that letter, it will still end. So why do it?'

"I'm ashamed of being single, I have to admit it. I have grown to hate the word. It makes me feel inadequate. The worst thing someone can say is, 'How come you're still not married?' It's like saying, 'What's wrong with you?' I look at women who are frumpy and physically undesirable and they're monochromatic and uninteresting and they don't seem unselfish and giving and I wonder, 'How did they become such an integral part of a man's life that he wanted to marry them and spend his life with them?' I'm envious. They're married and I date.

"When I think of dating, I think of Saturday night, not knowing what to wear, not knowing the person who's going to pick you up, of taking a drink to calm your nerves. I'm so aware of how I'm responding. Am I laughing too loudly? Am I laughing at the same places he's laughing? Am I having a good enough time? Were the tickets expensive? Do I seem appreciative enough? Should I have a drink at intermission or will he think I'm a gold digger?"

Claudia, twenty-five, is not playing in quite the same league as Jody. Her boyfriends take her to football games and picnics and visits with their mothers. But like Jody, she feels she has been through the whole process too, too many times.

"Every Sunday afternoon, my boyfriend's family watches football together," she says. "Three years ago I would have sat there, too. But I work forty hours a week. I've got two days to do my laundry, go grocery shopping, run errands, work out, see my friends, and at this point I don't have to watch him watch football anymore. I need to maintain my own life. I've had three serious boyfriends since I was nineteen and I'm not giving away the shop anymore. I'm not going to get close to someone else's family again unless it's the real thing. I don't want to kiss another Aunt Sadie because one week you're kissing them and the next week suddenly they're total strangers. When I have a ring on my finger, I'll kiss Aunt Sadie, not until then. I don't want to play the wife or the fiancée until I am one. Right now I'm still only a date. And dates are replaceable."

The "To Love or Not to Love" Debate

Let others [debate the most impor]tant issues our age: Will there ever be a nuclea[r ...] [up the] environment? Is Madonna pregnant? W[...] [issue clo]ser to home: Is it better to have loved [...] loved at all?

Karen vo[...]

At forty-[...] [wal]king cliche. I've lived every major trend of th[...] [Tr]end No. 1: She got married right out of college. [...] [had] two children. Trend No. 3: She celebrated [...] [annivers]ary with a divorce.

At thir[t...] [wor]k (Trend No. 4) and she started to date (Tren[...] eleven years she has had four significant relationships, many insignificant ones, and more dates than she cares to remember.

"I guess you could say that all those significant relationships ended badly because I never married any of the men, although at the time I wanted to. One was with a married man who wouldn't leave his wife. One was with a guy who dumped me for another woman. One was a long-distance romance with a man who didn't love me enough to rearrange his life. And one was with a man who just couldn't make a commitment.

"There was a lot of pain in all the endings and some resentment. I was better to every one of them than they were to me. And not one of them handled the breakup well. In fact, all but one of them just stopped calling —and this was after long, serious relationships where marriage had been discussed. The married man had his own way of ending it. He moved out of town.

"But all that aside, I wouldn't have missed one minute of it. Those are my memories. I didn't date much in high school or college and this is my past. When I'm an old lady, I'll have incredible memories.

"The married man was my first real lover—I don't count my husband —and he brought out a wild, passionate, fun-loving side of me that I didn't even know existed. He would hold me in his arms and sing to me. I would dress up for him. Once I met him wearing a raincoat with nothing underneath. I felt like I was a character in a cheap paperback and I loved it. It was a sweet, sexy, giddy affair and it was exactly what I needed. It gave me confidence in my womanliness.

"The guy that dumped me was the first man I ever really loved—again I don't count my husband. And he adored me, at least at first. I'll never forget the first time we met. There was such electricity it was like a current was passing back and forth between us. We'd go out to dinner and he'd sit across from me, drinking me in. I never knew how happy I could be just staring at someone's face. I really didn't know I was capable of that kind of love until him. It's a wonderful thing to learn about yourself.

"The long-distance guy was so irresponsible, but he could always make me laugh. I never knew people really missed planes until I met him. He did it regularly. Once we were going to meet in Miami and drive to Key West together. We were supposed to meet at the airport, rent a car, and off we'd go. But I knew him a little by then, so we had contingency plans. Just in case he didn't make his flight, we were supposed to meet at the Howard Johnson Hotel on Biscayne Boulevard. Well, it turns out there are two of them. I checked into one, waited around, fuming, and finally ordered a room service dinner. He waltzed in about midnight. I was ready to kill him so he knew he had to turn on the charm in a hurry. He made me get dressed and we went to the Boom-Boom Room in the Fontainebleau Hotel. We danced and danced and wound up staying up all night and watching the sun come up. I'll never forget that night.

"But my all-time favorite was the guy who couldn't commit. He made me feel young. Having children while I was still a baby made me grow up too soon. He was just a year younger than me, but he lived and acted like a kid. He dressed in jeans and sweatshirts and I started to dress the same way. We'd sit around a neighborhood bar and play the jukebox on Saturday afternoons and have a couple of beers. I know it sounds incredible, but I'd never done that before in my life. It was like he gave me back my youth.

"It's funny, but as time goes by, I find the memory of the pain has dulled, but the memory of the good times just get sharper."

Is there a cure for these social diseases? Sure. Love. It's penicillin for the heart. Just wait till Donna falls in love, then you'll see how fast her cartons get unpacked. Wait until John meets the right woman. It won't take him long to get back into dating. Just let Vanessa meet the right man and watch her give celibacy back to the nuns. There are a lot of new social diseases out there, but fortunately, few of the ones we've mentioned are fatal.

6

I Knew It Was Love When . . .

There are a lot of blatant indicators of love—trips to Europe, two-carat baubles, Valentines written in the sky—but there are more discreet and wonderful signs as well:

- He realizes his lover is his best friend.
- She's able to eat a full meal in front of him.
- He wants to stay in bed with her until noon on Sunday instead of going running in the park.
- She says, "I love you" before he says it first.

Just so you won't waste any more time wondering if this is really love, take the *Tales from the Front* True-Love Test and find out for yourself.

For Women Only

1. Has he put a child seat on the back of his bicycle for your son?
2. Have you thrown away the letters from your high school sweetheart and burned your diaries?
3. Did he tell you he had absolutely no desire to see the nude pictures of Vanna White in *Playboy?*
4. Did he babysit for your daughter and even change her diapers?
5. Did he give away his burgundy, black, and white patent leather shoes because you hate them?
6. Did he teach you about football because he insisted it was more fun to watch in the living room with you than at the local bar with his buddies?
7. Do you think those little snores are cute?
8. Did he ask you out for a third date after you showed up wearing braces on the second?
9. Do you wait for Stop signs to turn green?
10. Have you shaved your legs twice in one day?

For Men Only

1. Have you held her hand in front of your mother?
2. Has she held your hand in front of her father?
3. Does she laugh at your jokes, even when you suddenly realize you've told them already?
4. Do you sing in front of her?
5. Do you tell her when you're scared?
6. Have you invited her to leave her hair dryer at your place?

7. Do you think she's beautiful first thing in the morning?

8. Have you come out the other end of three major fights still thinking she's the best there is?

9. Would you switch to the other side of your bed for her?

10. Have you agreed to see her astrologer?

If you answered *yes* to half of the questions, you've got something good going. Keep at it, but don't throw away your little black book yet or cross out any of the names with a heavy marker. If you answered yes to at least eight questions, you may have to pop the question tonight. Don't let this one get away. If you answered yes to all ten of the items, you are already married to this person. You must be. You are wrong if you think there is someone better for you.

Here are some other things we've heard you say about that special feeling that love is here at last.

I knew it was love when . . .

• he helped me wallpaper three rooms of my new condo and we were still on speaking terms afterward.

• he asked me if I had to go to the bathroom before we went on a long car ride, and during it too.

• I told him I couldn't make a date one Friday night because I was going to wash and wax the floor and he offered to come over and help.

• we got tired of saying "Your place or mine?" and wanted an ours.

• I looked at other attractively dressed women and tried to visualize how good she would look in those outfits.

• I woke up to find he had folded all the laundry.

• he took me fishing and didn't pout when I caught the biggest fish.

• she asked me for one of my baby pictures.

• she said she would go see a Czechoslovakian film I wanted to see on our first date.

• he said he could picture us as old grandparents as much in love as when we first met.

• on our second date it was 3 A.M., we were at his apartment, and he didn't say he was too tired to drive me home.

• I admitted to him that I only iron the cuffs and collars of blouses that I wear under sweaters. It was something I had never told anyone else before.

• I suddenly wondered what I had seen in my last boyfriend.

• she thought some of my less desirable features were "cute."

• he gave me his childhood teddy bear for safekeeping.

• we took separate vacations and called each other every day.

• I would get a letter from him and my heart would pound so that I couldn't open it.

• I arrived early for a date and saw her with her head in a dryer hood and her feet in a footbath and still thought she looked good.

• I could make funny faces and talk to myself in front of the mirror and not worry that she would think I was goofy.

• he spent an afternoon playing softball with my eight-year-old sister, who drives me crazy.

• we were on our way to a Ray Charles concert. My boyfriend and I were in the backseat. His best buddy, George, and George's girlfriend were in the front seat. Suddenly George looked into the rearview mirror and winked at me. I winked back. The next day he came over to visit, told me my boyfriend was engaged to another girl, and asked if we could go out. Three months later we were married. That was seventeen years ago.

• I asked him, "What was your major in college?" and he told me that he had two degrees. One was in invertebrate biology and one in civil engineering. He added that by virtue of his education the only thing that he was really qualified to do was build zoos for insects. It was love at first speak.

• the going got tough and my lover didn't get going. I broke my leg in a parachuting accident and I was totally helpless. Rather than back away from lots of problems, Don dug in and took care of business. Above and beyond the call of duty he stayed with me, fed me, bathed me and even walked my dog. What a special guy. Before he left for work in the morning he made coffee, got me the morning papers, set me up for the day with the TV remote control, pillows, etc. After work it was grocery shopping, dinner, errands, and anything I wanted or needed. We've had our share of ups and downs since the accident, but I can hardly remember the downs.

• I was playing the cello at rehearsal and I happened to look over at Steve, the principal bassist, and I was overcome by an incredibly hot, prickly sensation from my head to my toes. It was very difficult to play for several minutes so I just enjoyed the feeling and faked several pages of Beethoven's Fifth. That was six years ago and we are still making great music together.

• my husband and I were vacationing up north after we had been married for about five years. It got extremely cold and the heat gave out. When I got up in the morning, he was nowhere in the cabin. I called and heard his voice coming from the bathroom. "Hurry up," he said. "Come in here." And there he was, sitting on the john fully dressed, keeping the seat warm for me. If all goes well we will celebrate our fiftieth anniversary this coming summer. It all seems like yesterday.

• I was willing to quit my job, uproot my child, and leave my family and friends to live in London with him. The next time I knew it was love was when I was willing to do all of the above for another guy who lived in New York. This time I'm sure it's love because I'm prepared to do it for a man who lives in Milwaukee.

7

Holidays

Holidays can do strange things to a relationship. Such as make it or break it. Sure, a holiday is just another day of the year (the way thirty is just another birthday). But all too often it becomes a litmus test of a romance. Is your birthday the lucky day you find a ring tucked inside a velvet box? Or a pair of thermal socks? Is New Year's Eve the night the two of you vow to ring out every old year together and herald in every new one side by side? Or the night it suddenly hits you that you could never build a future with anyone who looks like that in a party hat and can't do the limbo? Was Valentine's Day the first time your shy sweetheart whispered "I love you" and handed you a box of your favorite milk chocolate–covered caramels? Or was it the day you suddenly realized that if you want this much pain in your life you might as well stick your hand in your Cuisinart?

Of course it's probably true that relationships are really made up of ordinary Mondays and Tuesdays and Wednesdays, but when all is said and done, it's the holidays we remember.

Birthdays

Allison's marriage is an example of one relationship that works great 364 days a year. But on her birthday, watch out! The problem is that she expects a day that's a combination of Valentine's Day, Christmas, and the Fourth of July all wrapped in one (large) bright, shiny, beribboned package—and she's married to a Hallmark, sign-it-quick kind of a guy.

The trouble is, she grew up in a family that made a big deal out of birthdays. "I always had a big party with lots of excitement, lots of kids, lots of presents," she says. "It was a major social event. To me your birthday is your own personal holiday. It's a perfectly wonderful, selfish, 'Hey, I was born today!' day and I think it should be treated as such."

Unfortunately Sam, Allison's husband of eight years, does not feel the same way. He thinks birthdays are the occasion to give your spouse that cute little power drill or that sexy little paint roller she has had her eye on all year long—"utterly practical, Sears kinds of gifts," she calls them —and then get on with life.

"A couple of years ago he gave me two bargain-basement pots and a knife. I was ready to use them on him. I wanted a personal gift from him:

jewelry, a scarf, an item of clothing, a book, perfume. Something that would symbolize, 'You're special.' "

Allison is not one to suffer in silence. She has explained to Sam several times—usually on the day *after* her birthday—just how important the day is to her and how she would like to be treated. "It has gotten to the point that each year as my birthday approaches he becomes more and more anxiety-ridden. He wants to do the right thing and he never does."

This year is a perfect example. Together Allison and Sam planned a birthday party for her—a bowling party for forty people. So Sam figured this year he was off the hook. Wrong! Allison woke up bright and early and Sam's first words were, "What are you making for breakfast?" Then he left the dirty dishes for her to clean up and went out. There was no card, no wacky little gift waiting beside the scrambled eggs.

In the middle of the day Allison burst into tears. Then Sam burst into tears. He said he was trying so hard to make the party come off that he was a bundle of nerves. Allison said that one big-bang event wasn't enough. She needed the little stuff, the thoughtful gestures, the special treatment. Where were they?

She dried her tears and went out. When she got back, there were some carnations waiting. But Allison calls them "guilt flowers" and says she got no satisfaction from them. "I had to yell and cry to get them."

What will become of Allison and Sam? Neither seems willing or able to budge. "I don't know if it's an emotional death wish on his part or a power trip on my part," she says. "I always feel incredibly trivial and stupid when it's over. Here I am stamping my feet and saying, 'You don't give me flowers!' I'm demanding little material gestures instead of looking at the big picture. This man loves me deeply. It's so stupid and so immature. I don't know why it's such a big deal to me. It just is."

Allison isn't the only woman to have irrational feelings about her birthday. Heather says, "The day I got a beautiful birthday gift but no card was the day I knew it was over." Becky adds, "I waited all day and night for him to call or send me a birthday present. By 11:30 P.M. there was no call or special delivery. I was so upset that I called a friend and we talked for two hours. I got off the phone around 2 A.M. and waited for an hour more and finally went to bed. He called the next day and said he had tried to call me and got a busy signal. Now he was mad at *me*. He said he was so mad that he tore up the birthday card he had made for me."

And then there was Rose. She told us, "My thirty-first birthday started out like just another day. You know how it is, you wake up and feel so special and then there's a gradual, almost embarrassing letdown when other people are acting like it's just another morning. You want to say, 'Wait a minute, August 11 is not just another day, it's not just the day the Mets won, or whatever, it's my birthday!' Anyway, I was going out with someone who had never really let me know how he felt about me or the relationship.

"We had been dating for three months but I hadn't been able to read him. I guess early on I had mentioned when my birthday was, but I hadn't expected him to remember. I vowed that I wasn't going to tell him on the day itself even though we had a dinner date because that would put him in a tough spot if he had forgotten, which I assumed he had. He took me out to dinner and at dessert pulled out a box with a gorgeous bracelet inside. He gave me a card, and signed it 'Love.' We're still dating a year later and now he can say out loud the word that he first wrote on the night of my birthday."

Maybe whoever said it's not the gift that counts it's the thought was only half right. Apparently it's both.

Valentine's Day

Valentine's Day was the red-letter holiday for Charles and Mary. Both in their mid-twenties, they had been dating for about a month when they were invited to a Valentine's Day party hosted by a few of Mary's high school friends. Along with the other guests they drank a lot of heart-red punch, ate from a plate of heart-shaped cookies, and played the usual party games: charades, truth or consequences. Then the hostess came up with another great idea. Each guest was invited to write a poem to his or her partner. Charles, suddenly inspired, quickly dashed off the following red-hot verse:

> When I was a young lad I dreamed ahead
> To the day when I would wed
> A Jayne Mansfield, a Marilyn Monroe
> An Elizabeth Taylor or a Brigitte Bardot.
> I found my dream girl to be none of these,
> But an irresistible creature with 32Bs.
>
> I love you for your body.
> I love you for your head.
> But most of all I love you
> Because you're great in bed.

Then the poems were put into sealed envelopes and everyone had to pull one out and read it aloud while the other guests tried to guess who had written it. For some strange reason everyone instantly knew that Charles was the author of this sonnet. Mary was humiliated and the two had "quite a scene" on the way home that night.

Fortunately her sense of humor returned the next day. They talked and she forgave him. In fact, she proposed to him. They were married one month later and that was twenty-three years, three kids, and many love poems ago.

But that original poem is still a hot topic of conversation. Friends from the party have not forgotten it. In fact, the only people in Charles and Mary's circle who don't know about it are their children. Showing them the poem would only shatter a lot of illusions.

"We'll show it to them someday," Charles says. "But not now. Right now we're having enough trouble telling them not to rush into relationships."

New Year's Eve

New Year's Eve is another holiday that can have a major impact on a relationship. There are so many expectations attached to the night. Not only are you supposed to have a date, it has to be a Serious Date. We know one woman who sets herself the goal of having her New Year's Eve date locked up by Thanksgiving. So much significance is attached to that one long night—maybe because it bridges two years—that whole relationships have been known to crumble and fall on the basis of how the night turns out.

Everybody seems to have memories of that one overblown holiday:

Vernon, who's divorced, remembers New Year's Eve 1982 this way: "We were bar-hopping with my wife's sister. At about 1 A.M. some guy asked my wife to dance, a slow dance. And she did. Well, that was all I needed to see. An argument followed, during which my wife and I both dredged up things about our marriage. It got rather loud and people were looking at us, still wearing our paper hats. My wife and her sister took a cab home and I slept in the car. We communicated via notes for about two days and separated in April. We were divorced a year and a half later. Happy New Year."

Debbie is also divorced; this is how she remembers New Year's Eve 1984: "My husband and I drove downtown for dinner at a fancy restaurant. It was nice but not too thrilling. Then, instead of going out for drinks, we went straight home. I turned on the TV to watch the annual festivities and uncorked a bottle of champagne we had saved for the occasion. I was still dressed up. My husband disappeared into the bedroom and emerged a few minutes later dressed in jeans and a T-shirt and clutching a wad of sandpaper. 'I think I'll finish sanding the table,' he said. So he spent the rest of the night sanding. I sat in front of the TV consuming an entire bottle of champagne, dressed to kill and ready to do just about that."

But New Year's Eve can also be the greatest night of the two years it straddles. It can be the start of something besides a brand new calendar:

The way Scrooge felt about Christmas, that's the way Tina felt about New Year's Eve. Ever since she could remember, she hated it. Even as a child, when there was no pressure to have a date, she still dreaded it. There was just something about that holiday that made her sad.

For a long time she managed to get sick every New Year's Eve. When she was a kid, her neighbors would host a gala midnight soiree—the event of the year—but she never made it. She would be in the house with a fever, watching the merrymakers through her window, tears streaming down her face. "Everyone else in my family was at the party and I was home, miserable."

And then she hit her teens. Her opinion didn't change although she did manage to stay healthy, more or less. Some years she would actually go to a party; other years she would stay home. It didn't seem to make any difference. As she says, "The outcome was the same: I was alone."

The final straw was the New Year's Eve her brother was home from the Coast Guard. He volunteered to escort her to a party. For reasons known only to those who have been aboard a ship for a very long time, he drank himself silly. The night was a disaster. Tina vowed that from that point on she would never even try to have a good time on December 31.

She was out of high school by this time and working in a hotel restaurant. December rolled around and she volunteered to work New Year's Eve. As long as she was going to have a "lonely, depressing night" she figured she might as well get paid for it.

So Tina was the hostess at The Prime Rib that night. The place was jammed—all those people blowing their horns, throwing their confetti, eating their medium-rare, and pretending to be having the time of their lives. When the place finally closed down, Tina went up to the nightclub to help out there for a while. She's not exactly sure where she was when midnight rolled around. It wasn't a big deal. Maybe she got a "peck on the cheek" from a coworker. Maybe not.

As the night wore on, the team of employees who had worked so hard grabbed some drinks and headed for the back of The Prime Rib. Sitting across from Tina was Mr. Rado, the restaurant manager. He was older (twenty-six) and Tina and the other employees had been instructed to call him "Mister."

Mr. Rado was "quite handsome" and Tina had had a thing for him for some time. But she never dreamed it was reciprocal.

As they sat around laughing and talking about the night and the clowns who had been in the restaurant, Tina caught Mr. Rado giving her a look that was not that of a grateful boss to a faithful, hard-working employee. There was a certain glimmer in his eye. Tina returned the glimmer.

As he was locking up the restaurant, Mr. Rado handed her a room key and said, "I've got a bottle of Rebel Yell. Would you like to help me drink it?" Tina hesitated for a microsecond and said, "I guess."

Well, that was in 1978. Tina and Bob—she calls him that now—have spent every New Year's Eve together since. She is now Mrs. Rado and sometimes she gets a shiver when she thinks how close she came to having another lousy New Year's Eve that year. It turns out that at the same time that Mr. Rado was making eyes at her, he was playing footsie under the table with another Prime Rib waitress. She could have gotten the Rebel Yell line, and Tina would have chalked up another lonely New Year's Eve.

Thanksgiving

Even Thanksgiving, a holiday more often associated with already in-tact families than blooming or wilting couples, has spawned its share of romantic tales, some about love amid the sweet potatoes and others more like this one:

It happened because nobody should ever be alone on Thanksgiving. Everyone should be sitting at some dining room table, passing the stuff-ing, eating the turkey, asking for seconds, declining the pumpkin pie. That's certainly the way Glen felt about it, so when he met Lainey, who was absolutely, stunningly beautiful and who also had nowhere to go for the holiday, he decided to bring her home.

He had met her only a week before, at a party. He was there with a date, so he didn't ask Lainey out right away although he was kind of bowled over. He felt that would be unfair to his date. Instead, he looked her up the next night, they talked, and he discovered that she had no family in the area. Even though it would be their first date, she was thrilled to spend the holiday with Glen's large, boisterous family. She arrived at his mother's house with a dozen roses.

So far so good.

"Lainey fit in, she was at ease," Glen says. "She came in, headed straight for the kitchen, and was suddenly side by side with my mom, preparing food, setting the table. It was incredible. Mom, of course, thought the world of her. A first date taken to a major family event can be disastrous, but this looked good."

The large crowd finally sat down to eat.

Glen, who is thirty, has five sisters. One of them had brought a thirty-five-year-old friend of hers named Allen, whom she was interested in, for the holiday as well.

Glen was sitting in between Lainey, his date, and Allen, his sister's date. Early on in the meal, Lainey, who is thirty-three and a masseuse, and Allen struck up a conversation. A good one. So good, in fact, that they strained their necks to talk over, behind, and around Glen.

"I almost felt an impulse to lean back so they could talk across me," Glen says. "When I would go about my business and eat my dinner, at a certain point they were trying to maneuver their faces around my head so they could see each other."

Glen wasn't sure how to react. And besides, it was a first date with Lainey, right? What rights did he have? What could he really say? He didn't say anything.

After the meal the trio—that's Glen, Lainey, and Allen—adjourned to the TV room for a football game. This time Lainey landed in the middle of the couch. Glen was on one side, Allen was on the other.

"Picture this," Glen says. "She is in the middle of the couch, leaning to her right. He is to her right with one hand right next to her leg—*this* close—and his leg was crossed, and by twisting, he was directly over her. He was pretty darn close, as a matter of fact. A lot closer to her than I was."

Still Glen held his tongue.

"It was borderline—enough to send off alarms all over the place but not so much that I could comfortably say, 'Uh, Allen, would you mind peeling yourself off my date?' "

Finally it was time for Allen to leave. Glen was relieved, obviously, until Lainey called to Allen from across the house, "Oh, Allen, did you want my number for that massage?"

Right.

Allen came bounding back and sent Glen in search of a pen. Great, Glen was thinking, here I am helping them hook up. Lainey gave Allen her telephone number in front of Glen, his mother, and his sister (the one who had been hoping to date Allen). When Glen dropped Lainey at her place that night, she said something about getting together again. Glen just muttered. That night a relative called him on the phone.

"Uh, Glen," she said. "I don't know if you noticed, but I think you've got a problem with your date. I hope you weren't planning on a long-term thing with her."

Glen said no. And just to make sure he wouldn't give in to any small, overriding impulse to call her again—she was, after all, a beauty—he ripped up her telephone number into little tiny pieces and threw them away.

Christmas

When all is said and done, the best holiday tale we ever heard offers a trace of the supernatural and a truckload of hope and good cheer. It is one of the best holiday tales of all time—in our opinion second only to "Yes Virginia, there is a Santa Claus."

It was last year during the holiday season. Esther was sitting all alone in a crummy little neighborhood theater, watching a crummy little play and shivering. It was freezing outside and inside too. She sat there in her coat, her scarf wound around her neck, her mittens on her fingers. She was due at a party later that night, but as the play droned on and her fingers went numb she drearily wondered, "Why bother?"

"There I was thinking to myself, 'This is my life. This is what it has come to. I'm past thirty-five, I've never been married, I'll probably never get married. It's the holidays and I'm all alone watching this miserable little play."

So she decided to go home. She got undressed, took off her makeup, and climbed into bed. And then she heard a voice. It wasn't a mugger. It was the voice of her grandmother, who was no longer alive. The voice clearly said to her, "Get up, put on your prettiest dress, and go to the party. Keep trying."

Now, if your grandmother's voice comes to you with a message from the other side, you are going to listen to it. And this was no ordinary grandmother. Esther's grandmother, who had raised her, was a very, very wise woman. She had all kinds of wise sayings. She used to say, for instance, that life is like a jar of instant coffee. When we first get the jar, we put way too much coffee in each cup because we think the jar will last forever. But as we get down to the bottom we start to get stingy with that coffee. We want it to last and last and last—but we also realize that it won't.

Esther listened to the voice. She got up, got dressed, put her makeup back on. As she walked to her car, she slipped and almost killed herself. "It was so snowy and slippery out." She was the last one to arrive at the party, but within five minutes a "quite adorable, darling, very handsome" man started to stare at her. And not just stare; he absolutely burned a hole through her with his eyes.

"I said to myself, 'This isn't happening to me.' My face flushed and my heart started to beat. I thought there must be food dribbling down my chin. I went into the kitchen to start clearing plates and he followed me."

It turned out that the adorable stranger, Patrick, had seen her several days earlier in a restaurant and had said to the people he was with, "I would love to meet that woman." Patrick asked Esther if she remembered him from that night. Esther thought fast. She said she hadn't been wearing her glasses that night so she hadn't seen him. But that if she *had* seen him, she wouldn't have forgotten him.

"I wanted to send him a clear-cut signal that I was interested in him. He took a risk with me and I wanted to let him know I was worth it."

The party lasted until five in the morning. Esther and Patrick sat and talked all night long. "We had a wonderful, easygoing time."

The next day he called and asked Esther out for New Year's Eve.

"We went out with several other couples, but I have no recollection of anyone being there," she says. "It was like being in a movie. It was love and it was total insanity. I had never known it in my whole life. I'm a scientist and there's nothing that I have ever studied that had prepared me for anything like this."

Since New Year's Eve, Esther and Patrick have been nearly inseparable. He proposed on her birthday nine months later and it was a day as special as the day they met—although this time there were no voices other than his and hers. He kept her out of the house all day—being pampered at the beauty shop, massaged, manicured, pedicured. When she came home, he blindfolded her and led her into the bedroom, where there was a new long black evening dress waiting for her with all the accessories. When she was dressed, he blindfolded her again and led her into the living room. He took off the blindfold and as far as she could see

---

there were roses and candles. Patrick was wearing a tuxedo. He got down on his knees and said, "I want to take all the time in the world to tell you I love you."

"We were both crying," she says. "I thought we would faint. He took out a ring and said, 'I would be honored if you would spend the rest of your life with me.' "

They got married one year from the day they met. And now, every day is a holiday.

8

Mixed Romances

Diahann Carroll marries Vic Damone and nobody blinks. Diana Ross says "I do" to a Norwegian shipping magnate and everyone wishes them well. Black and white couples barely get a second glance these days.

But there are mixed romances that can still make people stare. We're talking about the Blue-Collar/White-Collar Romance. You see these couples everywhere. Ann Jillian married her bodyguard. So did Patty Hearst. Ditto Susan Ford. They all get a snicker in polite society. But do they care? Don't bet on it. Neither does Sherry, a high-powered media buyer who fell in love with Gus, a steel salesman. She gets her hair coiffed at a high-priced salon. He gets his hair cut in a barber shop in a bowling alley.

We're talking Older Women/Younger Men Relationships, too. Here's to you, Mrs. Robinson. You knew a good thing when you saw him. You were just ahead of your time. When Anne Bancroft put the moves on Dustin Hoffman in *The Graduate,* it was shocking. Now everyone's doing it. Have you seen Mary Tyler Moore's husband? He barely shaves. What about Olivia Newton-John's? He must get carded in bars. Even Debra Winger robbed the cradle for Timothy Hutton. Older women obviously have something going for them, besides a healthy bank account.

And then there's the Oil/Water Mix. Just look around you. How many couples do you see and wonder, "What could they possibly have in common?" The answer is frequently, "Nothing." Not a blasted thing. They don't like the same movies; they don't eat the same foods. They don't have a middle ground, and for them, that's sometimes the best thing they've got going.

Blue Collar/White Collar

When Muffy, "the quintessential yuppie," met Jake, "the ultimate working-class stiff," her friends got very nervous.

Muffy is a twenty-eight-year-old stockbroker and a self-described "snob" with a group of about ten close women friends. Snobs all. They're graduates of fancy business schools. All consultants, investment bankers, and CPAs. All "cute, bright, fun to be with, and really intelligent," according to Muffy. They're all committed to their high-powered careers, but they all expect to marry someday, too.

Unfortunately, most of them don't date much. In fact, they spend a good deal of time "lamenting the dearth of 'good men.' " You know who the "good men" are. Those are the ones who are "committed to their work, open to the idea of marriage and family, and possessed of a good sense of humor."

Well, lucky Muffy actually met one of those "good men." Jake is a salesman. He comes from a working-class neighborhood. His clothes come from Sears.

He wasn't like the usual men Muffy dated. Most of those guys abused her. Not physically, but emotionally. They'd say they'd call; they wouldn't. They'd forget her birthday. "The typical garbage," says Muffy.

Not Jake. He treats Muffy the way she's always dreamed of being treated. He listens; he cares; he remembers. "He makes me feel safe and more cherished than any man I've ever known," she says.

So she decided to bring him to a little party of about thirty of her closest friends.

"He was nervous. Here he was, your basic blue-collar Irish Catholic, surrounded by all these Waspy swells. He was the only one there who was actually born in Chicago. He was as out of place as I had been in my little fur coat and my little Guess jeans at Ryan's Daughter or Ryan's Hope or Ryan's whatever, that Irish bar he likes."

Perhaps it was only Jake's nerves that caused him to commit some truly unforgivable faux pas that night. His sins were legion. Where do we start? First of all, he asked for a beer when everyone else was drinking white wine. He wore a worn turtleneck while everyone else had just removed the Polo tags from their clothing. He smoked.

On the other hand, he did not pinch the hostess. He did not eat with his hands. He did not tell dirty jokes. He never put a lamp shade on his head. He got into no fist fights. He slandered no one's mother, sister, girlfriend, or wife. He insulted no one's ancestry. But it was too late. He had already done enough.

The beer, the cigarette, the turtleneck.

"The next day at least half of the people who had been at the party called to give me their impressions. They all said that they felt they just *had* to let me know that they thought Jake 'lacked polish' or 'seemed loud' or 'might not be a suitable match,'" Muffy says.

Now, you may think that Muffy's friends are simply very sensitive, demanding people. A group of princes and princesses who can detect a pea under the fluffiest stack of mattresses. But you'd be wrong. Actually, they've been quite accepting of some of the other men that Muffy has brought to their little parties. Or should we call them inquisitions? Winston, for example, was a great favorite.

"He got drunk, ignored me, and asked for other women's phone numbers right in front of me. But he was six-foot-four, the classic preppie, with blond hair, horn-rimmed glasses, and Ralph Lauren clothes."

And most important of all, he didn't ask for a Pabst Blue Ribbon.

So now Muffy is confused. "Jake is the first guy I've been out with in a long time that I've really liked. I was excited about him and my friends knew that. I was surprised by their reaction. I'll admit there's some validity to all their comments, but it's hard to express how violent it was. It made me think about what these women really want in a man. Whatever they say, what they *really* want is someone they can take to a business dinner. They want someone who comes with a tux. Like a Ken doll."

Muffy may have come to a crossroads in her young life. It's clear that there's no way she can bring Jake among her friends for a while.

"I don't want their reaction to muddy my feelings until I get them sorted out," she says.

It just may be time for Muffy to choose between her man and her friends.

Is there *really* any choice?

While Muffy is making up her mind, Roseanne, a thirty-six-year-old college professor with a Ph.D. in history, has already made up hers. She's having the time of her life with Stan, an auto mechanic.

On the surface, they don't have much in common. She shops at high-class department stores; he favors K mart and Venture. She's dovish on military spending; his philosophy is "Bombs away." He has never used the word "yuppie," never eaten a Lean Cuisine, and thinks a Dove Bar is something you use in the shower. In spite of all of it, Stan and Roseanne are in love.

They met at a singles' party seven months ago. He asked her to dance. She said, "Why not?" They had a great time that night and he asked if she'd like to go out sometime. She said, "Sure." He asked her out again. She went, but she wondered if she should continue with this. They really didn't have much in common, after all. So she turned down his next invitation. But then she found herself missing him. She called him back, and they've seen each other about four times a week ever since. They've even talked about marriage.

"I'm very attracted to him," says Roseanne. "He's very masculine. He's sexy. The chemistry is right."

She likes the fact that he can do the physical things that the professional men she has dated couldn't—or wouldn't—do. Unclog a drain, rotate her tires, connect her VCR. She doesn't mind his double negatives anymore, although they used to drive her crazy. She doesn't care that he refuses to help with the cooking or the laundry even though her ex-husband dutifully shared those chores.

They have a rich, down-to-earth life together. He has introduced her to his world. They bowl. She hadn't bowled since high school. They've been canoeing. They go to mom-and-pop restaurants in the suburbs instead of overpriced, trendy, high-tech places with eyedropper portions. He'd laugh at them. They don't get into the city much. "We haven't been to the art museum or the symphony," she says with some regret, but not much.

She finds herself doting on him.

"I'll go to Burger King myself so I won't have to wash dishes, then he'll come over and I'll cook something for him," she says with surprise. "It's something I would never have done for any other man. Maybe I'm nuts, but I guess it's because I really like him and he gives me a tremendous amount of affection. It's a small price to pay."

This is not to say that all is perfect. Sometimes small problems arise when Roseanne has to grade papers at night or prepare a lecture. Stan becomes jealous. He's an auto mechanic. When he punches out, his time is his own.

"He thinks of his job in terms of hours and I think of mine in terms of getting the work done. Our views on discipline are very different, too. He's much stricter. It seems to me that professional people are more into behavior modification whereas blue-collar people think you should just spank. If my son does something wrong, I tend to say to him, 'No TV tomorrow.' My boyfriend would rather just spank him and get it over with."

Every once in a while, Roseanne thinks maybe the relationship has gone about as far as it can and she should break it off, a thought that makes her feel like a terrible snob. But usually she has no problem introducing Stan around. Here's where she has a big advantage over Muffy. Six of Roseanne's friends are in, or have been in, the same position.

"One is a Ph.D. who married a cop. Another has a master's degree in social work and she married a fireman. Another, a professor, married a postal worker. And it's not because of any male shortage. It's just nice not to have to compete intellectually. But what's much more important is just being able to have fun with someone."

Are we making it sound as if all blue-collar/white-collar romances go in only one direction? We don't mean to. In fact, Josh, a twenty-nine-year-old, very white-collar businessman, is a little amused that women think they're on to something new. He thinks it's kind of cute the way successful professional women are getting all hot and bothered over working-class guys, acting as if they've discovered something slightly forbidden.

"This is not a recent phenomenon," says Josh. "Men have known about it for years."

Josh and his friends, professionals all, bluntly admit that they prefer dating waitresses, cashiers, and store clerks to lawyers, doctors, insurance agents, and schoolteachers. This despite the fact that it invariably invites comments from professional female friends along the lines of, "You could do so much better."

"I feel like responding, 'She is not *just* a secretary or *just* a waitress or *just* a file clerk. She is also a warm, caring, considerate woman who is fun to be around,'" Josh says.

But aren't there any warm, caring, considerate, fun-to-be-around *professional* women?

Josh doesn't seem to think so. He has dated them for years and he says he has learned, the hard way, that if he wants a noncompetitive, noncombative relationship, he has a better chance of finding it with a nonprofessional woman. And besides, he says, he doesn't feel any particular need to discuss foreign affairs or economic theories when he gets off work.

"It's not that I'm looking for a nonopinionated, passive woman. But it is disconcerting to me that so many professional women between twenty-six and thirty-six have failed to recognize that it is not a compromise of one's self-worth or womanhood to be feminine, sexy, flexible, and just plain nice when they're around men.

"I enjoy doting on my dates. Yet when I've opened a car door for a professional woman, I've been told, rather strongly, 'I can get that myself.' Why do so many professional women feel that they have to compete? I'm in a very goal-oriented competitive environment every day at work. I don't want to compete when I go home."

One professional woman Josh dated couldn't stand that he beat her at tennis. "For some reason she needed to be my equal. So she went out and unbeknownst to me she took lessons. Then she asked me if I wanted to play again."

Josh wants to make it clear that he's not interested in some dingbat.

He doesn't like to date women who are unemployed because he admires a certain "get up and go" spirit. But he just doesn't think it matters much whether someone takes pride in keeping her work station clean or her ledgers straight.

He'd love to discuss this at some length, but he has to run. A few nights ago, he met a wonderful young woman in a bar. They talked about values and goals and life. And all while she kept everyone's glass filled, made change, and mopped the bar. She's going off-duty in a couple of minutes and Josh wants to be there to pick her up.

To Josh, Roseanne, and Muffy, the wrong side of the tracks is the right side.

Older Women/Younger Men

Let us now praise older women. Daniel is an all-night disc jockey at a radio station. He first discovered the allure of "the older woman" when he was a mere lad of sixteen. He fell for a well-seasoned woman of nineteen. She was his first date—to this day he still doesn't know why she accepted his invitation—and she will remain forever etched in his memory.

"She had so much to teach me," Daniel says. And she did. So when a recent live-in relationship ended, Daniel went out again in search of the older woman.

He found himself at a friendly neighborhood bar and he fell in with a group of women in their forties. He's twenty-eight. Since then he has spent every Friday night, his only night off, with them.

"Probably the biggest reason I feel so comfortable with them is that they're nonthreatening. They don't care about my income because they're financially stable. They don't care what kind of car I drive because they own new cars themselves. They don't care whether or not I live at a prestigious address because they have their own beautiful homes. They like me for who I am.

"These women are themselves and they aren't so hung up on what other people think of them, a lesson I'm taking to heart. They dress the way they want, go the places they desire, and act the way they do to please themselves."

Daniel says when they all get together they have some great no-holds-barred conversations and he has learned a lot about women from them. They've learned a couple of things about men, too.

"Our conversations sometimes remind me a little of the high school locker room. They can get pretty braggy and detailed. I love talking about my passions to them. They love to hear how men look at women. They in turn tell me what they look for in men. They're all very special to me. I have them coded into my speed-phone. They were touched by that."

For the moment, the relationships between Daniel and his older women are platonic. They're all buddies. But he's not ruling anything out. "I'm not looking to fall in love with any one of them, although it's happened in the past and just may happen again."

Daniel's not the only man who's turned on by gray hair and a couple of stretch marks. Mark, forty-three, a city planner, has dated women from nineteen to their late sixties. And he says he prefers the grandmothers to the teenagers.

"Older women are sexy," Mark explains simply. "They know something about themselves—their minds, their hearts, and their bodies. They're softer where younger women still have hard places and rough edges. Older women even show this in their physical appearance. The wrinkles, the crow's-feet, the graying hair. All these are evidence of women having lived long enough to have experienced life, of having loved and lost perhaps, and loved again. To me, this is far preferable to the look that many younger women seek—the look of being in mint condition. To my eye, this appears fake, hollow, plastic, and dishonest and gives the effect of being a character in Madame Tussaud's wax museum.

"Finally, let's get something straight about older women and eroticism. I don't know where Western culture got the idea that sexiness is limited to younger women, but it's just not true."

And that's from a man who's in a position to know.

Oil and Water

Arnie and Claire are completely, entirely, and totally different.
• He comes from a small Southern town. She's a big-city girl.
• They have never read one book in common.
• They eat different foods. Arnie grew up on grits. Claire has barely learned to *look* at grits, let alone eat them. She passes when he fixes one of his favorite dishes: ketchup over black-eyed peas over corn bread. He is wary of her women's magazine recipes. Things like tuna tetrazzini and three-layer jello molds.
• They listen to different music (she wore earplugs when he took her to

a rock and roll concert) and at different volumes. "He cranks the stereo up to where I can hear it when I'm driving down the street and up to the house," Claire says. "The first thing I do when I walk in is to turn it down. That's how he knows I'm home."

• Given a little free time, Claire will choose a romantic movie and Arnie will opt for sci-fi. Arnie likes computer magazines. The ones Claire likes he calls *"Better Housekeeping* and all that."

• She's a talker; he's not. Sometimes the silence drives her buggy. He'll be reading one of his computer magazines and she'll come sit on his lap, on top of an ad for floppy disks, and say, "Talk to me."

And that's the least of it.

These are two people whose thermostats are set at opposite poles. Claire is hyper and charged up most of the time. Arnie's the laid-back type. His philosophy is, "Things will get done when they get done and if they don't, well . . ."

They don't even like to sleep the same way. "She's got to have the sheet and blanket tucked in nice and tight," says Arnie. "I'll pull up the sheet and that's about it. If a bed could have two different temperatures, ours would."

They're only grateful that Claire doesn't care much for politics. They figure the explosions over that would be too much.

So how does the marriage work?

Great!

"He's in first speed and I'm in fifth and most of the time we manage to meet in third," says Claire.

Each of them has his own way of getting there. "If I want something done and he's not doing it, I end up doing it myself," says Claire. "I've been after him to do the kitchen floor and he's been saying, 'I'll get around to it,' so I know that one of these days I'll just do it."

Arnie has developed his own way of dealing with his super-charged wife. When she's on one of her tears, he leaves the room or goes for a walk. "He basically won't let me pick a fight with him," says Claire. "He'll listen to me and then go about life at his own pace."

It's the differences that keep this marriage cooking, not the cooking. Arnie and Claire know that if they were ever to appear on "The Newlywed Game," they would get the lowest score on record. Fortunately, being on "The Newlywed Game" is not one of their goals in life. Having a marriage that lasts forever is. They think they've got a pretty good shot at it.

Arnie and Claire aren't the only couple with precious little in common. On paper, Maureen and Sandy are about as similar as Kathleen Turner and Pee-Wee Herman.

They met at a singles dance. Maureen had just moved to the big city and didn't know a soul. When she saw an ad for the party, she went with the highest of hopes.

She was so disappointed. One clod after another crossed her path. When yet another one came up and said, "Has anyone ever told you that you look exactly like Mary Tyler Moore?" she just about lost it. This was the last straw. She was about to say, "Stuff it," grab her coat, and leave. But she looked up to see exactly who the unimaginative dumb cluck was and that, as she says, was "it." They danced once, and then talked for a couple of hours over the noise. They were both hoarse for days.

On paper, it didn't look like a perfect match. Sandy was thirty-four, a big blond, husky guy. Maureen's mother calls him "a young Dick Butkus." He's a happy-go-lucky bachelor, the outgoing "good buddy" type, and a high school teacher who had just gotten his law degree at night.

"He's the kind of guy who goes to the Auto Show and meets people there he knows," says Maureen. "He specializes in putting down Eastern preppie snobs."

Maureen, twenty-one, was—guess what?—an Eastern preppie, a Wellesley graduate to be exact, and not a snob, but an admitted nerd.

"I'm quiet and shy," she says. "He likes buxom domestic women. I'm tall and thin, not much in the figure department, and a horrendous housekeeper." Not only was she not domestic, she was working in a bank by day, studying for her MBA at night. That schedule didn't leave much time for embroidering doilies or baking brownies.

They never could quite figure out if they were attracted to each other in spite of the obvious differences or because of them. All they knew for sure was that the attraction was there. In spades. After six months they got engaged and after another six months, they married.

It's never dull around their house.

"We argue about almost everything," says Maureen. "He's a rip-roaring Democrat and I'm a card-carrying Republican. We usually wind up staying home because we can rarely agree on what to do. He likes seeing things like museums. I prefer sedentary things like movies. He humored me last summer by taking me to the park to ride the paddle boats and then he didn't talk to me for three days afterward. I have one friend he likes, the others he barely tolerates. I don't like any of his friends."

Needless to say, when this happy couple gets their two weeks off each summer, their hands don't instinctively grab for the same travel brochure. "My idea of a vacation is lying on a beach," says Maureen. "Sandy would love to train-hop through Europe."

But compromise is the key to their happiness. So for their vacation this year, they've decided (for Maureen's sake) to visit her family back East. They'll stay with her parents, her two "hyperactive" teenage siblings, and the family's three dogs. (Sandy hates dogs.) For Sandy's sake, they're making the nineteen-hour trip in a sleeping car.

"I'm sure people who look at us must think we're lonely," says Maureen. "We don't have many friends, we don't go out much, but the secret is we're very content with each other."

And who can argue with that?

Is there a moral to this chapter? Is there a lesson to be learned? If there is, it's something like this: Phi Beta Kappas should try hanging around with garage mechanics, middle-aged women should start scoping young life guards, and bookworms should give it a try with guys who do magic tricks at parties. What have they got to lose?

9

Modern Fairy Tales

There comes a point when most of us give up the old fairy tales that put us to sleep in our youth: "Hansel and Gretel," "Goldilocks and the Three Bears," "Snow White," "Sleeping Beauty." But that doesn't mean that we're through with fairy tales. Not by a long shot.

We just substitute modern ones for the old standbys. There's the "I'll Call" myth. How many women have foolishly assumed that when a man said, "I'll call," he meant, "I will pick up my phone and dial your number. You will answer, we will talk, I will ask you for a date, and then we will take it from there." When all he really meant was, *"Byyyye."*

There's the Ghost Story. Have you ever been involved with someone who was only half there for you, just barely going through the motions, because he or she was waiting for some ghost from the past to resurface? This person gives himself away by being unusually fond of old *Topper* movies and collecting Casper comic books. He or she may have refused to see *Ghostbusters,* but sat through *Heaven Can Wait* five times.

There's the "Hey, I Don't Play Games!" fable. This is where we assume that everyone is playing it straight and that kindness is rewarded in kind. This is where we honestly believe that all those little tricks our mothers taught us are hopelessly out of date. This is where we find out— the hard way—that people are still playing games, but not everyone has the same set of rules.

There's the Fool's Gold legend. How many women who can spot a designer original even with the label cut out *still* get taken by guys who look better than they are? How many men who can instinctively tell a good business deal from a bad one still fall for women who present a good package, even when they have nothing to deliver? Learning that all that glitters is not gold can be a tough lesson, especially when that shiny object is your wedding ring.

There's the Dating Is Fun! tall tale. Prepubescent girls believe this with all their hearts. They dream about their first date: who he'll be, where they'll go, what they'll wear, even down to what they'll order at the soda shop. One young girl decided when she was about eleven that she'd have a tuna fish sandwich and a 7-Up on her first date. It was the most feminine thing she could imagine ordering. If pressed, she'd manage to eat a few spoonfuls of raspberry sherbet for dessert. It's a nice daydream. But somewhere into their first or second or third decade of nonstop dating, most people give up the illusion that Dating Is Fun!

"I Have No Wife" is one of the most popular modern fairy tales. Every cheater tries to use this line or a variation on it which can include everything from "My wife is dead" to "My wife is frigid." The gig is usually up when that dead, frigid, or nonexistent wife gets pregnant.

"I'll Call"

There is always that Moment of Truth on a first date. It comes at the end of the evening and usually occurs in front of the woman's front door. A signal must be given at this point—a sign, something!—as to whether or not the couple will have a future together—or at least a second date. And any parting comment that falls between "I know this is fast, but will you marry me?" on the one hand, and "Have a nice life," on the other, can be hell.

"I had a fine time. You've got a hearty handshake," is a stiletto in a woman's heart. "See ya," is like asking her to open a vein. But the worst possible ending to a first-and-last date?

"I'll call you."

At this very moment, millions of women are waiting for their phones to ring. They're telling their girlfriends they can't talk, they've got to leave the line open. They're postponing picking up the cleaning and walking the dog. They're declining invitations to wine tastings. All because of three hastily uttered and totally empty words: "I'll call you."

Why do men do it?

Here's the reason:

"I had always heard from women that one of the things that bothered them the most was when men said, 'I'll call,' and then didn't," says

Doug, a twenty-eight-year-old suburban warehouse worker. "Then one time I found myself doing it and I felt terrible about it."

Part of the problem, Doug says, is that first date beginnings are eased along by small talk—"How long have you worked there?" "Do you have any kids?" "Where did you go to school?" Standard questions and social scripts. But first date *endings* are different. There's not much left to say. Each party just stands there, desperately trying to read the other's mind.

"I know that rejections are best when they're clean and swift," Doug says. But that's only in theory. The reality is quite different. "It's hard to reject a woman to her face. So men say 'I'll call' for the same reason that women lie when they turn you down for a date with the usual response: 'Oh, I'm busy then. Maybe some other night.'

"When a woman says that, in your heart you know that she's probably trying to be nice and let you down easy, but there's always a little nagging voice that says, 'Gee, suppose she really *is* busy and she really *does* want me to ask her out another time.' If you're like most guys, you wait a week or two, ask her out again, and when she turns you down again, you slap your forehead and say, 'Why did I do that?'

"Saying what you don't mean is cowardly and we all, men and women, scream about how much we hate it. But do we really want the truth? Would you really prefer it if at the end of a date the man turned to you and said, 'I didn't have that good a time. I don't want to see you again'? Sure, talk of honesty comes cheap. Being able to face it is tough."

A friend of Doug's has arrived at a solution.

"Early on in the first date, you casually ask the person if they want kids," explains Doug. "If you've decided you don't want to see the person again, you say the opposite of whatever they've said about the issue.

If they say, 'No, I don't think so,' you say, 'Oh, I want four.' Then you drop the subject. At the end of the date you say, 'You're really nice, but it's really important to me to have kids, so I don't think this relationship could ever work out,' or else 'I had a wonderful time, but I wouldn't dream of bringing a child into a world with acid rain so I guess we don't have much of a future.' And then you say good-bye."

Kind of makes you nostalgic for the good old "I'll call," doesn't it?

"Hey, I Don't Play Games!"

Did you ever take Psych 101? Remember those rats in those cages? The ones that hit a little bar in exchange for a pellet of food? There were a few different groups of the little guys. One group pressed the bar but never got any food and they quit pushing real fast. The second group got food every time and they ate themselves into a little frenzy. But when the food stopped, they stopped hitting the bar. Then there was the third group. Sometimes they got food when they hit the bar and sometimes they didn't. And you know what? They'd keep tapping away on that bar forever, hoping they'd get lucky again.

Which brings us to relationships. Researchers call what the last group got intermittent reinforcement. You don't give them what they want all the time—you give it to them some of the time. And you can keep their interest forever.

Which brings us to Liz. When Liz is in love, she tries to be the perfect girlfriend. Loving. Warm. Supportive.

"If I'm dating someone, the last thing I want to do is hurt him. I'd never insult him in front of his friends or make fun of his favorite old sweater. If he's having a rough time at work, I'll offer to take him out to dinner or send him a red rose or bake him some brownies. I'll listen all night if he wants to talk. And I get dumped all the time."

This is precisely what happened when Liz, twenty-seven, a publicist, dated Mitchell, twenty-seven, a middle manager.

"He was having a lot of trouble with his boss, who just didn't respect him. So when we went to office functions, I'd play the charming girlfriend, putting in a good word with his boss, casually mentioning how much he loved his job and how hard he worked."

Naturally, Mitchell broke up with Liz for Rita, a whole different breed of woman.

"I saw them together at one of those office functions and I heard her put Mitchell down in front of his boss. She would openly abuse him. At a party, not only would she flirt, she'd brazenly give her number to other men right in front of him. She'd roll her eyes and groan every time he said something foolish. She'd stand him up for dates and never apologize. He'd call me up to talk because he said she never had time for him."

And he was nuts about her.

What's going on here?

Liz and her friends have a theory. "It seems if you love somebody as he is, then he hasn't achieved anything. But if you play hard to get, if you reject him, if you make him win you over, he feels like he's getting a prize. Guys seem to thrive on this kind of stuff. The nicer you are to them, the more they take you for granted. The less eligible you are, the harder they'll work to keep you. But who wants to play that kind of game?"

We're through with all that game playing, aren't we? It went out with teasing your hair. Or did it? I think that's the way it works," says Victoria, a woman who considers herself an expert in relationships. "It's like the old law of supply and demand. If you make yourself plentiful, your value or your price goes down. If you keep yourself in short supply, your value goes up. You're a commodity. You might as well face it."

Do you doubt that it's true? Think about what happens when you're in a restaurant. You're debating whether to have the linguini with clam sauce or the fettucini alfredo. You can't make up your mind. You go back and forth. You finally decide on the linguini. And then the waiter says, "Sorry we're all out. I just served the last order." All of a sudden, you *crave* that linguini! Victoria would advise you to, every now and then, be the linguini.

"People need drama in a romance," she says. "And drama is built on conflict. If you're nice all the time, you're predictable, and let's face it, that's boring. You need to create some tension to keep someone's interest. Allow yourself to not always be so loving and supportive. It's okay to do something nasty every now and then. In fact, it's necessary."

Victoria actually has a nice-to-nasty formula worked out. For every nine times you say, "Gee, honey, you look tired. Let me get you that beer," she suggests one zinger. One "Get up and get it yourself," or "Don't kiss me, you need a shave," one phone call unreturned, one stand-up.

"I'm not saying I like playing games," says Victoria, "I just think it's worth thinking about."

The Ghost Story

Greg doesn't mind competing for a woman's affection with a man who's taller than he is, a man who's smarter, a man who's better-looking, or richer, or even more charming. He has his own assets and they're nothing to sneeze at. He thinks he can make it a fair fight and hold his own.

But there's one man he can't compete with and, ironically, it's the one he finds himself most often pitted against: The Ghost.

Greg, thirty-six, a playwright, says ghosts are old boyfriends who keep women from getting involved with anyone else. Namely him.

He has run into this particular challenge several times.

"The women are all attractive, intelligent, and talented, but they're also emotionally off-center," he says. "They're playing with maybe fifty-one cards in the deck, three quarters of their oars in the water. Most of them happen to be actresses, but I don't think it necessarily says anything about actresses. Because of what I do, it seems that that's all I run into. But I believe women in lots of other occupations are pretty much the same, holding on to these shadow figures."

Greg has some theories about these women. "They've grown up with an idealized view of love, that there's only one person in the world who's right for them. Most of us grow up at a certain point and realize there is more than one person we can love and who can love us. But these women don't."

He also has some theories about the men, the ghosts these women can't let go of. "They're all very macho guys who don't give very much of themselves. They don't share their feelings. They certainly weren't as much in love as the women were. Several of them were described to me in almost exactly the same words. They're the Marlboro Man type, rugged, classically good-looking. One woman summed up one of these guys by saying, 'He's just a *real* man.' "

You can imagine how terrific that made Greg feel. What is he? Chopped liver?

The first woman who read Greg the Ghost Story was Vicky. She had dated her phantom, Bob, for five years, but only casually. She was in love with him and she knew that someday he would "come to his senses" and love her in return. She spent several months with Greg, but finally gave him up to wait around full-time for Bob to "see the light."

Then there was Sandy. She had a Bob in her past, too. (Greg has named all these ghosts "Bob" because he's convinced they must be the same person.) Sandy and Bob had dated hot-and-heavy for a couple of years before he broke up with her. She dated Greg for a while, but finally she broke it off, too. She wanted to save herself for Bob, on the off-chance that he might decide to return sometime. Anytime.

Greg was introduced to Linda by mutual friends. She, too, had a "Bob" tucked away. They just dated occasionally, but she was waiting for Bob to "get serious" about her.

"I know that their friends and relatives have told these women that they're wasting their time, but they always say that they know these guys better than anyone else does and that someday they'll give in to their real feelings—that it's destiny."

"You can't compete with these guys," adds Greg. "When I'm dating someone, I'm very affectionate. I like to buy silly gifts for no reason, send flowers. I always remember birthdays and anniversaries. I was dating one woman and she said to me, 'You treat me so well, I just wish Bob would treat me this way.' I just thought to myself, 'Oh, good, heap a little more on me.'

"But the truth is, these guys have a big advantage over the rest of us. We all know that when we're involved with a real, live person, that person may disappoint us. They may not be everything that we hoped they'd be. But you never have to worry about a ghost. He's never going to show up, so you're never going to be disappointed."

Fool's Gold

Some of the most discriminating people, the ones who have gold American Express cards, drink imported champagne, and can tell the difference between Coke and Pepsi, still get taken. They don't judge books by their covers, but they do choose potential partners by their trappings: a good job, a nice apartment, a great body. In other words, they fall for Fool's Gold.

Marnie was one of them. She describes herself as an "attractive, intelligent, successful, independent woman," a communications consultant, divorced, generally "a happy person." Shortly before her thirtieth birthday she went into a minor panic: Where was her one true love already? She decided to place a personal ad to nudge him along.

She got eighty-three responses. (She says it was a very clever ad.) But one really caught her eye. It was a snapshot with a yellow Post-it note on the back saying, "Hate to write, love to talk. If you're interested, give me a call." So she did. She called on a Friday. They made a date for Monday night. On Sunday afternoon, Mr. Post-it (his name is Scott; he's thirty-seven and owns a securities firm) called.

"I had mentioned on Friday when we talked that I liked riding in fast cars and he said he was in my neighborhood in his Ferrari, how about going for a ride? I thought he was joking, but I said sure, I had an hour to kill. I actually did have plans for later that afternoon and evening. Sure enough, he showed up in this little Ferrari. We went for a ride and we just hit it off. I wound up forgetting about my plans. We drove around and really got to know each other. We talked about our likes and dislikes, we discussed our dreams. Finally he pulled up in front of a huge mansion. I said, 'Where are we?' He said, 'My house.' I couldn't believe it. We went into this incredible seventeen-room palace and we had a great time. When I finally said I was tired and I wanted to get home, he called a limousine."

Pretty heady stuff, you'll have to admit. A Ferrari. A mansion. A limousine. What could come next?

Monday night they went out again. This was right after Easter and Marnie mentioned that she liked bunnies. On Tuesday an enormous bouquet of yellow and white roses and a huge stuffed bunny were delivered to her office.

"We were together every night for a month. We'd talk on the phone a couple of times a day. If I didn't call him, he'd leave messages on my answering machine saying, 'Remember me?' He liked me to stay over at his house, so he bought me a complete change of clothing to keep there: a suit, shoes, you name it."

Marnie's thirtieth birthday rolled around. She had mentioned to Scott that she had never been to New York, so he flew her there for a four-day celebration. They went to Atlantic City. They helicoptered over to Manhattan. They saw Broadway shows and toasted each other with champagne. When she got home, there were thirty roses waiting for her.

Sounds too good to be true, doesn't it? Marnie thought so, too.

"I knew I was hooked. The whole thing was dazzling. It wasn't that I was all that impressed with money, but I admit it was exciting, the places he took me, the things he bought me. But it was all so fast. I was afraid he'd get bored with me just as quickly as he fell for me. I was afraid of getting hurt. I told him I could handle anything, as long as he was honest with me."

Now we come to the second month. It was different.

"I started noticing changes in Scott. He was traveling a lot on business. The relationship seemed to be up one day, down the next. I said to him, 'Just tell me. Is it over?' But he kept saying no."

Now we come to the last month. It was horrible. Scott was pretty much AWOL for most of it. He had a lot of "business pressures" and "family obligations." He had very little time for Marnie. And when he did, she says she acted like "a total fool."

"He'd call me at maybe eight o'clock at night and say he wanted to see me. I'd pack a bag, just like that, and go off with him. I'd stay at his house where I never slept very well. He got up really early, so I'd be at work two hours before I had to be and then I'd drag around the rest of the day."

Toward the end of the disastrous third month, Scott made a date with Marnie. He broke it with a message on her answering machine. He never called back. Marnie waited a week and then she called him. There was dead silence on his end of the line.

She said, "You can't talk?"

He said, "Right."

And that was just about it. Except for a couple of cards. The first card Marnie sent Scott had a sexy woman body builder on the front. Inside it said, "No more Ms. Nice Guy." She wrote him a little message reminding him that he always used to say that he liked to leave all his doors open and she supposed she was just another door that had been left ajar and that one of these days he might catch a very bad draft.

No response.

So then she sent him a second card. This one was a birthday card, with a line that said something about how "Memories are our most cherished possessions" and inside she wrote that it was time to let bygones be bygones, and if he ever needed a friend, he should call.

No response.

So she called him. A woman answered. She hung up.

Marnie was dazzled by fool's gold. She's not the only one to learn firsthand that all fairy tales don't end happily ever after.

Jane fell into the same trap. She bought the sizzle and then found out that there was no steak. She should have known better.

When you've been divorced for nearly ten years and when you've dated a lot of men in that decade, you naturally assume you've developed some street smarts. That you can pick out the winners, smell the losers. Don't bet on it.

Jane, thirty-five, has knocked around since her mid-seventies divorce. "I think I know most of the single guys out there," she says. "I've had a few long-term relationships, and every time I came out of one, the pickings kept getting slimmer. That's why when this guy came along I knew I hit the jackpot."

Jane met him through work. She sells real estate and he was looking for a house. A big house. A very big house. A six-figure house. "For a single man of twenty-nine I thought that was a pretty decent purchase," says Jane. There was also "total instant chemistry" between them. "He was genuinely nice and he made me feel good. He was easy to talk to and he was so romantic. He sent me flowers all the time. He bought me a Concord watch a week after we started dating. We'd take walks along the beach. He owned a boat and we'd go out on the lake. He was wonderful to my son. They'd spend days together, going to amusement parks, riding bikes, going to movies. I thought he was perfect. I thought this is forever. Everything is great."

Well, not *everything*. Alex, the jackpot, had been married before. Three times. But, as Jane told herself, two of the marriages had been to the same woman, a Bible-toting Southern Baptist who was constantly trying to convert him, and the other was to a childhood sweetheart when he was just eighteen. He was also the overindulged son in a wealthy family with a father who handled him by saying, "Here's money. Go buy yourself a boat. It'll make you feel better."

Jane and Alex started dating in August. By October they were married. "His family was thrilled—I was solid, the same religion—and so was mine. They loved that I'd never have to worry about money again. It wasn't going to be 'poor Jane' anymore. We had a small wedding—just what we wanted. But as soon as I said, 'I do,' something cracked. He started leaving me on the honeymoon."

He walked out when Jane became annoyed because he wanted to

spend a lot of time with his sister and brother-in-law, who also just happened to be in Hawaii. He walked out when she objected to his friends calling them daily from the mainland. When they got back home, he walked out whenever he was angry, which was often. He raged against her son.

"At first I thought it was me. I lost sight of how proud of myself I had been and how independent. I blamed myself for everything. I had heard about his mood swings before we were married, but I had never seen them, and when I started to, I thought I was causing them. I never knew in the morning what the day would bring. I'd say to my son, 'Steer clear of him if he's in this mood, don't open your mouth if he's in that mood.' And then one day, he just told me he didn't want me anymore. I was like another one of his possessions that once he bought it and fixed it up, he sold it."

He left for good in March and now Jane's dating again. "Quantity, not quality" is how she sums up the men out there. But that's okay with her. She's not in any hurry.

"I've learned not to fall in love with romance. I have to lead more with my head than my heart. I'm looking for someone less romantic. I'm rearranging my priorities."

In other words, no there'll be no more Fool's Gold in her future.

Dating Is Fun!

You go out on a date with a new man. You come home. You call your best friend.

She says, "So?"

You say, "So what?"

"Don't give me that," she answers. "You know what I mean."

And you do.

She says, "Do you like him?" But that's not what she really means. What she *really* means is, "Do you think you could ever marry this man and live with him in a reasonably happy state for the rest of your life?"

Plus ça change, plus c'est la même chose, as the French say. The more things change, the more they stay the same. Even today, there's an unspoken rule that dating, exclusive dating, leads to marriage. Maybe not right now. Maybe not right away. Maybe we don't follow the same go steady–get engaged–get married path our parents wandered down. But sooner or later, like it or not, the expectation still exists that dating must lead to something other than more dating. That dating doesn't exist in a vacuum. That dating is a means to an end. And that the only real end, of course, is marriage.

Kara is twenty-five, a college graduate with a good job in the catering profession. She lives in her own apartment decorated creatively from the local assemble-your-own-furniture store and she dresses in Anne Klein II and Calvin Klein Classifications. She has lots of friends and lots of dates. However . . .

"All of a sudden all my friends are getting married and I'm getting nervous. You go to parties and everyone is discussing where they're registering and where they're having their showers and what band they've booked for the reception. And 'Did you get a marquis or a round stone?' and 'How many carats?' And they're all buying condos. That's Topic A of conversation."

She wants in on the action and she thinks she's figured out a way to beat the system. It all comes down to timing.

"You've got to get these guys when they're twenty-five," she insists. "No sooner and no later. By then they've been working for three years, and they've got a pretty large income coming in. They don't know what to do with it all. How many video games can they buy? So the next move is a condo, and why buy a one-bedroom when a two-bedroom isn't that much more and it's a much better investment. Everyone knows they appreciate faster and they're easier to sell when you're ready to move into a house. So they start looking around for a second income to help them swing that second bedroom—and that's when they think about a wife—and that's when you grab them.

"If they make it to twenty-eight, they start getting real comfortable with their income—they think of all kinds of ways to spend their extra money—and they learn to really love their lifestyle—the travel, the variety—and besides, they get real set in their ways. If they make it to thirty, forget it. While there's still another bar to go to or a new woman to sleep with, they've got to be there."

What would Kara have to say about Marty? He's twenty-seven, a perfectly happy-go-lucky bachelor. In fact, he has more women than some men have socks. He usually sees two or three at a time, sometimes more. He has a great time, so do they, and he thinks dating is wonderful. But always, in the back of his mind, is the notion that dating could and should lead to something more. . . .

"One woman I began dating recently let me know early on that she could never marry a man who wasn't Jewish and I'm not. Even though I had my reservations about her and didn't really think there was much of a chance that we'd get married, her announcement totally took the steam out of our relationship. All my fantasies were gone. I was unable to deal with a relationship that I knew, proof positive, had to end.

"Other times I've ended relationships after it became clear to me that no way did I want to live my life with this woman, no matter how delightful or attractive she was. This is often seen from the outside as me 'getting tired' of someone, and I'm chastised and I chastise myself for having a short attention span. But that isn't really it. It just seems unfair to me to keep something going when I know it's eventually going to end."

"I Have No Wife"

Mindy is a trusting soul. At first she refused to see the signals. When her husband, Jack, told her he was going to the hardware store to get some brackets—but he thought he'd take a shower first—she didn't think much about it. When he told her he had a Friday night business meeting that began at 9 P.M., she said fine.

When he didn't get home until four the next morning—because he had fallen asleep at his desk—well, stranger things have happened. But when his car started looking like a rolling bordello with lipsticks, panty hose, and stray earrings jabbed into the upholstery, she began to wonder.

And then she began to do more than wonder. She started checking the phone bill for out-of-town calls and going through Jack's pockets and wallet, looking for matchbooks and phone numbers. She found everything.

"I was taking his pants to the cleaners and I found a slip of paper with a name and work number on it, so I got the address and went over to see who it was. She was about forty-five, forty-six (Mindy is thirty-one; Jack is forty-two), a bleached blonde, heavy. Lately he's into older women. I said, 'Do you know my husband?' She said, 'No.' I said, 'Well, I found your name and phone number on a torn-off matchbook in his pocket.' She said, 'Oh,' and then she confessed. She told me they'd met at an over-forties hangout.

Other times Mindy has just called and sweetly said, "Hello. I'm Jack's wife. I think we ought to have a little chat."

This has happened so often that Mindy pretty much knows how the women will respond. "If they're dating a lot of guys, it will take them a minute or two to place him, but then they'll say, 'You mean he's married! He told me he was going through this traumatic divorce.' They're stunned. He's a very attractive guy, he drives a Lincoln Mark VII with a telephone, and he dresses beautifully. He comes across like a real catch. The women are devastated that he's got a wife."

After Mindy confronts the women, she confronts Jack. He denies everything. He's never heard of the women. He doesn't know how the stuff got into his car. All he did was have a couple of drinks. Deny, deny, deny. "And you almost have to believe him," Mindy says. "He seems so sincere."

Mindy knows Jack's haunts from his credit card receipts and she has made the rounds on a Friday night, trying to find him. "One night I barely missed him," she says.

Why, oh why, you wonder, does Mindy bother? It's hard to feel sorry for her. She has a choice. She knows what you mean.

"We've got a four-year-old and a four-month-old. I've got no other family in the state. We went to a marriage counselor once, but it didn't do any good. He swore he loved me and then I caught him cheating again a week later. He really doesn't think he has a problem. He thinks all married men fool around. But last Friday night my bags were finally packed. If he had been forty-five minutes later, I would have been gone. But what do you do with two kids at one-thirty in the morning? Check into a hotel?"

How do you answer Mindy? And what advice do you have for Janet?

It was one of those Sunday night singles dances in the disco of a big hotel and Janet was being hassled by the usual bunch of what she dismisses as "creeps and losers." She aloofly declined their invitations to dance and stood alone, radiating boredom and annoyance, when she felt that sensation you only get when someone is staring at you and has been for some time. She turned around to see a man she describes simply as "an absolutely gorgeous preppie-looking hunk."

The man with his eye on her was Michael and he wasn't part of the singles group at all. He was attending a three-day management seminar at the hotel and he had stopped in for a quick drink after checking in. He was thirty, from Nevada, divorced for a year, the father of a toddler. He and Janet talked some, danced some, talked some more, danced some more.

"There was an instant sizzling chemistry," says Janet, thirty-seven, also divorced, with one daughter.

"The next three nights were like something out of a romance novel. During the days he attended the seminar and I worked. But every night I drove to the hotel from my house in the suburbs and spent the night with him. Everything just clicked between us. We were so compatible, sharing the same views on love, goals, interests. . . ."

Alas. Even management seminars reach their closing presentations. On the last night Michael was in obvious pain. At dinner, he barely touched his surf 'n' turf.

"Janet," he said finally, "I love you."

But love is rarely easy. Especially for a man like Michael, who, as he explained somberly to Janet, believed so deeply in the sanctity of the family unit that he felt honor-bound to attempt a reconciliation with his ex-wife. He couldn't bear the thought of not seeing his son. Janet certainly understood this. She even admired it. Hadn't she raised a daughter all alone? Didn't she know how important it was for a child to have a father?

The two consoled each other and finally decided they had but three options.

"We decided the bottom line was (1) either run away and get married, (2) never contact each other again, or (3) correspond." They decided to (3) correspond.

They parted tearfully. A few days later she wrote him a rather lengthy letter. Then one day while she was at home she got a phone call from her cohorts at work. Michael had just called! She was to call him that night. Her friends, who had been filled in on every little detail of the romance, were betting he was calling to say, "Forget the other options! Let's get married!"

That night Janet reached Michael. What played out was not quite the scene she and her office companions had created so hopefully.

"He confessed that he was still married and that his wife had found the letter I wrote him. He also told me that his son wasn't a toddler, he was a three-month-old infant. And that this wasn't the first time he had cheated."

Janet didn't say much—she was in shock.

And about all she has to say about it now is, "I'm definitely not the naive type. I've been around and I can usually spot the married men. But this one . . ."

This one fooled her. She's too smart to believe she could ever be Cinderella and she knows her Prince is probably not coming. But she did wind up starring in her very own fairy tale anyway. She played the Chump to Michael, who took center stage in that familiar role: The Married Man.

We think these modern fairy tales will be around for a long, long time. How long? As long as men and women meet and fall in love, fall out of love, and start all over again.

And it's just possible that future generations of little boys and little girls will go to bed at night cuddling their teddies, stroking their blankies, and hearing their mommies and daddies read to them about the nice man who said, "I'll call" and never did or the pretty lady who swore, "I just love to date! Don't you?"

10

I Knew It Was Over
When . . .

You don't have to be the last to know. If you just know how to read them, there *are* telltale signs that the love light is no longer shining quite as brightly in your sweetie's eyes:
- She sees you on the street and keeps walking.
- He says, "Why?" when you tell him you love him.
- She folds your clothes and places them in a box outside her front door.
- He says, "Let's have lunch real soon."

To avoid the embarrassment of being the last to know when a relationship is over, take the *Tales from the Front* Dump Test.

For Women Only

1. Does he whisper, "Sherry, Sherry!" when you're making love? And is your name Susan?
2. The last time he slept over, did he take his toothbrush with him when he left?
3. Have you checked his phone lately? Is your number still on his automatic dialer?
4. Does his secretary ask your name and then say, "I'm sorry, he's in a meeting"?
5. Has he stopped closing the bathroom door?
6. Does he take the phone into another room before he uses it?
7. Have you found cigarette butts with lipstick stains on them in his apartment? And you don't smoke?
8. Have you stopped faking it, but he hasn't noticed?
9. Has he started signing his letters "Sincerely yours"?
10. Has he told you he's thinking about becoming a priest?

For Men Only

1. When you start to make love to her, does she say, "Get away from me"?
2. Has she tried to fix you up with her mother?
3. Has she suggested you go back to your ex-wife?
4. Has she started making you instant coffee?
5. Does her secretary treat you gently, as if you have an incurable disease?
6. When you start to tell a joke, does she say, "I've heard it"?

7. Does she yell, "I'll get it!" every time the phone rings?

8. Has she stopped shaving her legs?

9. Has she started wearing flannel pajamas?

10. Have you received an invitation to her wedding?

These are all danger signals. If you answered *yes* to half of the questions, your relationship is in serious trouble. If you answered *yes* to eight of them, your relationship is all over but the shouting, the crying, the moaning, the groaning, the throwing yourself at his or her feet, the tearing out of your hair, the beating of your breast, and the sticking of pins in a voodoo doll. If you answered *yes* to *all* of them, you have no relationship.

Here are some other indications:

I knew it was over when . . .

• I won a free trip to the Virgin Islands for two and he said, "Why don't you take your mother?" I knew it was *really* over when I replied, "What a great idea!"

• I heard her talk about me in the past tense.

• I drove thirty minutes from the suburbs to deliver some leftovers to my poor, overworked medical student boyfriend and when he saw me he said, "Oh, do you want to come in?"

• she fell asleep during a porno movie.

• I looked at him and thought, "God, are you fat!"

• I finally told him what I liked during sex and he still didn't do it.

• he called my contribution to our live-in relationship "rent."

• I realized the best thing we had going was memories.

• the kissing stopped and we went straight to sex.

• he referred to my "brown eyes." My eyes are green.

• I quit smoking and she didn't even notice.

• he suddenly started using all new expressions.

• she sent me a note asking that I return a paperback book—and she enclosed a stamped, self-addressed envelope to mail it in.

• I walked into his bedroom and found his ex-girlfriend's five-by-seven picture sitting on his dresser.

• she would glare at me and look like she was waiting for me to say something stupid every time I opened my mouth. I started apologizing to her before I even said anything.

• I opened up my VISA statement and noticed an unauthorized charge for $54. When I called the store, I discovered that my live-in boyfriend had used my card to send red roses to "Elizabeth."

• I heard a message on her answering machine from a man asking, "Have you told him yet?"

• I finally told him, "I *hate* sushi. I've always hated sushi."

• He watched me move a dresser by myself. I was five months pregnant.

• she beat me at arm wrestling.

• she went outside to pick up the newspaper and left the sports section in the driveway.

• I pulled into the garage and was glad his car wasn't there.

• I found out that someone was living in *our* apartment the five days a week I was traveling.

• I used the phone at his house and when I hung up he sprayed it with Lysol.

• he spent more time on a Sunday morning with his ex-wife than he had spent with me all week.

• he spent the time it took us to go from one place to another talking on the car phone with his friends.

• I finally realized I was happier when I wasn't with her. All she did was depress me.

• it hit me that I didn't love *him,* I loved who I wanted him to be.

• he said to me, "I know this girl, but we're only friends," and then I found out he was living with her.

• she called her mother instead of me to come fix her toaster.

• I found his old girlfriend's new phone number on his kitchen counter.

• his idea of fun was me watching him wash and wax his car.

• she started talking nicely about her ex-husband.

• she asked me how I felt about people with herpes.

• he started giving me gifts from the housewares section instead of Frederick's of Hollywood.

• after twenty-three years of marriage, I found canceled checks for a computer dating service and a motel room in our bank statement.

• he suddenly started ordering all these new foods in restaurants. Like pâté. He never ate pâté. He never even knew what it was.

• in a matter of twenty minutes, she said that she "loved" me but wasn't "in love" with me, that she was looking for the right guy to "totally" fall in love with, and that she was moving to California.

• I had to tell him it had been seven weeks since we had made love.

• I found two ticket stubs in his jacket.

• he didn't call and I didn't care.

• I stopped using "Mrs." in front of my name.

• all her friends started coming up to me saying, "It's too bad you two aren't seeing each other anymore." It was the first I had heard of it.

• after phoning him and chatting with him for a minute or two he said, "Well, thanks for calling."

We could go on forever. There are as many ways to tell when a relationship is over as there are relationships. And they're all different. But remember, it ain't over till it's over. For some satisfying tales of sweet revenge, read on.

11

Sweet Revenge

It's amazing how "I love you, I'll always love you" can turn overnight into "I despise you. I'll do whatever I can to make you miserable." It's incredible how people who have devoted themselves to making each other happy in every little way can become bitter enemies, turning their obsessive thoughts from "Will he call?" or "Does she love me?" to "How can I best ruin this person's life?"

Breaking up *is* hard to do, and it does strange things to people. Yesterday his happiness was contingent on hers. Today he can't get to sleep until he gets even. A week ago she was miserable if he was pouty. Today seeing a smile cross his face would kill her.

Everybody has his or her own personal brand of revenge: Some choose the old "I'll show him/her I don't care" routine, trudging bravely ahead with life. Some climb into bed, pull the covers up, surround themselves with Sara Lee and stay there for a week. This is the "I'll make him/her feel so guilty" variety. Some fall in love again immediately. Others stop at nothing short of public humiliation. One woman actually put together a *poster* of all the men who have done her wrong. A real-live poster filled with names, a kind of "least-wanted" list of the worst guys in town, the ones you need to avoid at all costs. Cross the street if you see one coming. Move out if one of them moves into your building. Change your route if one of them rides your bus.

Most tales of revenge aren't quite so public. But in their own way, each has done the trick.

A Loaf of Bread, a Jug of Wine, and a Scissors

For seven years Shelley, a school teacher, and Dave, a dental student, dated. Not in the sense of once a week, off-again, on-again, now-you-see-me, now-you-don't dating. No, it was steady, constant dating. Weekdays, weekends, holidays, family functions, vacations. Dave wanted to hurry up and get married, but Shelley, who was twenty-four at the beginning of the relationship, wanted to do it right. She insisted that first he finish dental school.

"Suddenly a year before his graduation he decided that he needed a new woman," Shelley says. "We broke up and he started going with someone else immediately. I was devastated. I couldn't eat. I couldn't deal with it. It went on for eight weeks."

Dave soon was miserable too and decided it was time to patch things up with Shelley. He rented a new apartment, one that would accommodate all her furniture, and planned a wonderful reunion weekend for the two of them in Wisconsin.

"He thought we would fall into each other's arms and live happily ever after," she says. "But love doesn't often work that way" and making up isn't usually that simple. "From the minute he picked me up, nothing went right."

The things that were wrong with the relationship before were still wrong. In fact, very little was right.

On the drive home from Wisconsin, Shelley was a basket case. This up-and-down stuff was too much for her. Before their reunion, Dave had mentioned that he had made plans for a Florida trip with another woman, one he had been seeing before his rapprochement with Shelley. Now Shelley was certain that he would in fact go through with the trip since their own short vacation in Wisconsin had turned into such a fiasco.

"In the morning I called him and he didn't answer," she says. "So I knew he had left for Florida. I was in a rage, but somehow I made it through the week. Then when he was back from Florida, I went over to the office where he had a night practice. I told him I wanted to talk to him at his apartment and that I would go there and wait. There were other people around so he quietly gave me his keys."

There is something you should know about Shelley at this point. She is an expert seamstress. And something you should know about Dave is that he is a hard-to-fit clothes horse. In the seven long years they dated

Shelley had made him an entire wardrobe: pants, shorts, suits, sports coats, and jackets.

"I would buy beautiful designer fabric and make everything," she says. "Everything was monogrammed and lined and hand-finished. Terry cloth robes. Sweaters and warm-up suits. Everything."

Well, Shelley took his keys and marched over to his apartment with a bottle of wine and a pair of scissors. She made one simple, distinctive cut in an impossible-to-disguise location on each pair of pants and across the front of each shirt, blazer, and suit coat. She went through his laundry and snipped up the dirty stuff. She went through the clothes lying on the chair for the cleaners. She wiped out his entire wardrobe.

"It had always been a joke between us that if he ever hurt me I would cut up his pants," Shelley says. "So when he came in, I just said to him, 'Well, the joke's not a joke anymore.'"

Before she went through with it, Shelley had discussed her plans for revenge with her therapist.

"He said it would be a self-destructive act because I had made all those things, but I felt it was a great thing to do. I got it all out right there.

"Later on his mother called me and said, 'Why didn't you slash the leather luggage you bought him or his tires, or smash his windshield?' But I didn't have anything to do with those items. His clothes had my love in them. They were me, and he couldn't have them anymore."

This tale has a postscript. Shelley has told this story to all the men she has been involved with since Dave. And when the time comes to break up with her, they do it . . . gently.

Take This Shopping Bag and Shove It

Joanne works in a huge downtown department store. She's a salesperson in men's fragrances. She and a group of employees, both men and women, hang out together. They have lunch together, go on breaks together, make plans for after work and weekends.

Chris, her boss, is part of that group too. After several of these friendly get-togethers he made it clear to her that he would like to be more than just friends. Joanne made it just as clear that she wouldn't. She had had some office romances and considered them an all-around bad scene.

"Everyone always knows what's happening. Men like to talk too much, and when it's over, you can't just walk away from it. You have to see the people everyday."

But those are logical reasons. And what with the strong musk odor coming from her perfume counter and the natural physical attraction between her and Chris, in no time at all the two of them were inseparable.

"We would have lunch together, go on breaks together, he'd come over by my counter to talk, I'd go and find him. We'd go out after work four or five times a week and see each other on weekends too," Joanne says.

This marathon dating went on for three months and then one afternoon Joanne called and asked Chris if he was ready to take his break. He said no. He had too much work to do. Maybe tomorrow. He wasn't taking a break today. So Joanne went up to the employee cafeteria alone. She sat down and in walked Chris and another woman. And not just any woman. Renee was the store hussy. She worked in men's clothing and the word was she had a different guy picking her up after work every day. She was seeing several men who worked in the store and heaven knows how many who were gainfully employed elsewhere. Joanne and Chris had even discussed her once.

"I had said something to him like, 'I don't know why all the men think she's so attractive,'" says Joanne. "She had a nice body but she had no class and she really wasn't very pretty. I remember he seemed very defensive but I didn't think anything of it. When I saw them come in, I didn't know what to think. First I thought, 'Well, maybe he just got his work finished and bumped into her and they're having a nice friendly break. But then when they sat down, they sat next to each other, not across from each other like friends. That's when I knew there was something going on. I turned my back on them. I couldn't believe he was doing it right in front of me."

When the break was over, Joanne went back to her counter and called Chris. "We have to talk," she said.

He came over that night and explained that his relationship with Renee was strictly physical. It was Joanne he really cared about. But Joanne wasn't buying it.

The next day she arrived at work with a large shopping bag. It contained the flotsam and jetsam of a three-month relationship. The things he had left at her house as they had gotten closer: his shorts and socks, his records, tapes, and books. A toothbrush, a couple of sweaters, running shoes. Joanne took the escalator up to the second floor. She dumped the contents of the bag right out in front of Renee—and dozens of other people, including surprised customers—and said, "Here, give these to your friend."

Renee felt so embarrassed. When Chris heard about it, he felt humiliated. Joanne felt great!

Hold On to Your Keys

The moral of the tale about Joel is this: If you're not living with someone, do not give out your keys. Even if that special person in your life offers to water your plants, take in your mail, feed your cat, wash your clothes, and stock your refrigerator while you're gone, don't do it. If you know what's good for you, do not make that extra set of keys.

While Joel, who's now twenty-three, was in college he dated a beautiful, demanding woman for three and a half of those years, a woman he met in freshman English class, one he still calls "the love of my life." Her name was Charlotte. After three years she decided that the two of them should "date other people" as well as each other but she assured Joel that if anything serious developed with another man Joel would be the very first to know.

He was. One morning German class was canceled so Joel decided to drop in at Charlotte's apartment. In the more golden days of their relationship she had given him a key. When the relationship began to tarnish she never thought to ask for it back and Joel never thought to offer it. So on this hot August morning Joel put her key in the lock and let himself in.

"There was a truck out front," he says. A truck, it so happened, that had been parked there since the night before when Joel had just happened to drive by Charlotte's place. Inside there was no one in the living room. A bad sign. There was no one in the kitchen. A worse sign. Joel walked into the bedroom and there was Charlotte. And Charlotte was not alone.

"I think I said something childish like, 'Nice to have known you,' and walked out," Joel says.

He was there a grand total of about twenty seconds, but needless to say, he did not forget the face of Charlotte's new companion. For months he obsessed about her, him, it. "I couldn't eat, sleep, or concentrate," he says. He heard from friends that Charlotte and her new love, whose name was Ray, had become fairly serious. Then one night Joel was whiling away some time at a popular campus bar.

"The guy she had been with that unforgettable night came in and sat down a few stools away from me," Joel says. "My rage and curiosity were fighting each other and finally my curiosity won out. I asked him, 'Why are you here alone on a Saturday night?' Ray recognized me immediately. He jumped from his seat sensing a fight, which was ridiculous since he outweighed me by about forty pounds. Then after seeing no malice in my face, he returned to his stool and began to talk."

The two rivals discovered their rivalry was now a moot point. They shared their matching sorrow over a few beers. They didn't have much else to talk about, so they talked on and on about Charlotte.

"Ray began to confide in me," Joel says. "Men will confide in anyone when they're hurting. He told me he thought she was fooling around. He had asked her out for that night and she had said no, she was busy. Anyway, he had never really trusted her after being an eyewitness to how she and I finally split up."

Joel, generous sort that he was, ventured that there was one sure way to determine if this other man's gnawing suspicions were true.

"I offered him the key to her apartment," he says with some embarrassment but no remorse. "I still had it."

"Ray left the bar and twenty minutes later he returned," Joel says. "Tears were rolling from his eyes. He wasn't sobbing but he was definitely crying. Worse than I had been. I knew from the expression on his face what he had seen."

It had taken Joel a while to get his revenge, but he finally did. And it was worth it.

Keeping Tabs

Sam is a single, forty-eight-year-old blue-collar worker who has never been married. He is a simple man who leads a simple life in small-town Indiana. He has been dating for three decades during which time he has had six significant relationships, most of them with independent professional women. In every case the women have ended the relationships because they were looking for "someone better."

Ouch.

Sam was hurt by these endings. But he was still curious enough to keep track of how well these women have done. And for him revenge comes in discovering how they have fared in their search for that "someone better."

Woman No. 1 has been married twice, both times to "super, wonderful" guys who also turned out to be alcoholics. She is currently divorced.

Woman No. 2 has also been married twice, first to a man who abused her both mentally and physically and second to a man who was already married. She is also currently divorced.

Woman No. 3 married a "wonderful, charming" man who loved her "very deeply." Unfortunately he also loved several other women the same way and tried to prove it to each and every one of them. She is currently divorced.

Woman No. 4 married a man whose theme song was "I can't give you anything but love, baby." He brought no assets into the marriage, liquid or otherwise. Upon their divorce he helped himself to half of her property, including her house. She is currently divorced.

Woman No. 5 married a great guy who was also somewhat in debt. She cleaned up his back alimony and child support payments and finished paying off his Corvette as well. After a year she learned that he was still seeing his ex-wife. She divorced him after he took her for half of her home and property. She is currently divorced.

Woman No. 6 broke up with Sam several months ago, after four pretty good years together. They had even discussed marriage. She told Sam that he is a "wonderful, warm person" and that she would always have "a special place" in her heart for him. But now, nearly a year later, she is still looking for "someone better."

Sam will be watching her progress closely.

Sam describes himself as a one-woman man who has "never cheated or been abusive." He has always, he swears, "treated women with great respect and kindness and caring."

Because he lives in a small town he frequently runs into his former lovers. He can't help wondering if "not quite good enough" Sam doesn't look a little better now. But it doesn't matter if he does, although that thought makes him feel better. Sam says he is no longer available.

"I want to let all the women who are looking for someone or something 'a little better' know that there is one not-quite-good-enough guy who won't be in your way any longer. After about thirty years of this I am taking myself out of the dating scene. I am going to stay home and let you look for whomever or whatever you think is better. Good luck."

So Sam's out of the market, at least for now. The best revenge, as he sees it, is the revenge of subtraction. He says that with him gone there'll be one less man.

(Estranged) Americans in Paris

When the airlines invented tickets you have to pay for thirty days in advance, they forgot about the fickleness of love.

What happened here was that Sharon and Jack, who'd been dating for a year, decided to go on a vacation together. And not only a vacation, but the most romantic vacation of all time. They chose Paris, the most romantic destination in the world, and made their reservations at the most romantic hotels in the city.

They leafed through guidebooks together; they pored over maps. They read *A Moveable Feast* out loud to each other and talked about retracing Hemingway's steps together. They circled famous little restaurants on little Left Bank side streets in their Michelin guide. They talked about the galleries they would visit. They dreamed of the wine they would drink, the cheese they would eat on romantic excursions to the countryside. They bought their plane tickets.

And then a funny thing happened. Jack ended the relationship.

"Shortly after we bought our plane tickets—the kind you lose money on if you cancel out—Jack just stopped calling," Sharon says. "It was about three weeks before we were supposed to leave on this trip we had been talking about for months."

At first Sharon didn't know what was happening. She called him once and asked what he was doing that night. Jack said he was busy. After a few days word got back to Sharon that he was seeing someone else. The only trouble was he didn't know how to tell Sharon.

Sharon was heartbroken over losing Jack, but no matter what, she knew she was going to Paris. Years earlier she had studied at the Sorbonne for a year; she spoke fluent French, she knew the Metro better than the streets of her hometown, she had several close Parisian friends, and she needed a vacation. She was going, period.

The time of the trip quickly approached and one afternoon Jack called and said he wanted to see Sharon. When he showed up where she worked, her heart just about stopped beating.

He told Sharon that at first he had thought he could date both women. But he said that he realized that he was really a "romantic" who wanted to be in love and that he had fallen hard for the other woman. Then he said all those depressing things that women hate to hear: He liked Sharon; he never wanted to hurt her; he knew she would be okay. And at the end of his little speech he said, "Now, what about Paris?" The tickets were paid for, they'd lose money if they canceled, and after all, they got along. Could he and Sharon still go, as friends? (Another reason he didn't mention was that his new lover was married and not free to travel.) Sharon said that she didn't know about him, but that she was going.

"So the time came and we went together and the first thing he did at the airport was call his girlfriend," Sharon says. "But of course in my mind was this fantasy that once he saw how wonderful I was on this vacation, he would fall in love with me all over again."

Sharon *was* wonderful. She knew everything about Paris. She knew everything about the *suburbs* of Paris. She felt at home. But it turned out that this man she was in love with who was so smart and handsome was a terrible tourist. He couldn't read a map; he didn't speak a word of French. He couldn't translate dollars into francs without a calculator. He had lived his entire life in a triangle whose sides consisted of Chicago, Detroit, and Milwaukee.

Sharon, though, was in her element. It was as if she had never left. Soon after she and Jack had arrived, she phoned a good friend from her Sorbonne days, who told her to come right over; she said that her French cousin, Jean Pierre, was visiting and that she was sure he and Sharon would hit it off.

"I left Jack at the hotel and went over to see my old friend, who lived in a beautiful apartment, right off the Place de la Concorde," Sharon says. "I walked in and there was her cousin, the most fabulous-looking man you ever saw, with the sexiest accent in the world and the sweetest personality. We *did* hit it off. My friend told me that she was leaving the next day for her weekend home in Normandy, along with her cousin, and she insisted that I go too."

Sharon raced back to the hotel, threw some things into a bag, and told Jack she would be back in a few days. Jack spent that weekend glued to a chair at a café on the Champs Élysées, afraid he would get lost if he moved. He also saw a couple of American movies. Meanwhile, Sharon was in Normandy, eating mussels and drinking white wine with Jean Pierre.

"It was the greatest thing that could have happened. Here was this gorgeous guy making a big fuss over me, wining and dining me for the rest of the vacation even after we got back to Paris, and here was Jack kind of gawky and ill at ease in a foreign city," Sharon says.

"Now suddenly I felt in charge and good about myself, and I started really noticing all the little things I had never liked about Jack. The things I would never let myself admit, like how he looked goofy when he got a certain expression on his face, how he had a weird spring to his step I didn't like. I remember it was the first time I let myself say to him, 'You told me that,' when he started telling me a story he had already told me about a dozen times. On the plane coming home there was a subtle shift of power. We went over there with him holding all the cards, but we came home differently. I never saw Jean Pierre again, but I was over the hurt of Jack."

It might not be nice to dump someone's clothes in front of his new girlfriend. It may not be thoughtful to wipe out someone's entire wardrobe. It's probably not the most genteel thing to leave someone on their own in a foreign country. But to hear Joanne, Shelley, and Sharon tell it, sometimes it sure feels *good*.

12

Looking for Love in All the Wrong Places

People assume that because we write a column about love and romance we must know *everything* about these fascinating subjects. They assume we know all about how to hook someone, how to keep someone, and especially, how to meet someone.

But we don't have all the answers. We listen to you. *You* tell us where you're meeting people and we go out and check the action, then tell you what we found.

We've checked out the electronics department at a department store in Chicago. (We short-circuited.) We've stalked through the zoo. (Most of the cuddly critters we met were in cages.) We've been down and dirty in the laundromat. (The only thing we came home with was static cling.) We even struck out in a singles bar. (The only man we actually talked to was a neighbor's husband.)

The idea for these field studies came from a TV show that aired on ABC a couple of years ago. It was a special called "99 Ways to Attract a Man." The show promised women that they'd be overwhelmed by eligible men if only they'd use a little initiative. Naturally we paid attention.

First a sociologist gave lessons in flirting: Stand pigeon-toed. (It makes you look vulnerable, kind of like Annie Hall.) Surround yourself with a field of laughter. (Who couldn't use a good laugh?) Play with your hair and jewelry. (It calls attention and points him in the right directions.) Once you've gotten him within arm's length, touch him—in a non-threatening way. (In other words, don't grab.)

To prove how well this works, a group of women was unleashed at Bloomingdale's in New York, pointed toward the electronics department, and given one hour to get the phone number of a potential date. Most of the women beat the clock. They returned, not just with phone numbers, but with real, live men. One woman, all aglow, said, "They're so friendly and willing to talk to you! It's amazing!"

So, armed with the knowledge that men are truly "friendly and willing to talk," we set off for the electronics department of Marshall Field's in the heart of men-filled downtown in Chicago at 3 P.M. on a chilly Saturday afternoon.

We're reasonably attractive women. We assumed that anything a group of New York women could do, a couple of Chicagoans could do better. When we got to the electronics department, we separated. Better to case the joint.

"May I help you?" we were asked repeatedly as we moved from stereos to clock radios to cassette players to tape recorders.

"Just looking," we answered every time.

Looking at what? There was a group of Japanese tourists near the video cameras, watching themselves on TV. They obviously weren't going to be around long enough for a meaningful relationship. There were marauding groups of teenaged boys from the suburbs playing with the computers. They were on their own field trip. There were many couples arm in arm, shopping for VCRs and other symbols of rampant domesticity. There was one derelict in front of a wall of TVs, watching intently. And there was us. Where were all the single men?

Quick! There was one in front of the Home Entertainment Systems Center. He looked a little glassy-eyed, but we weren't in a position to be fussy. Cheryl sidled up. Side by side they watched a four-foot-tall dancing Mennen Speed Stick.

"Good reception!" said Cheryl sprightly, ending with a little chuckle (creating that all-important field of laughter). Her prey responded with a grunt. She moved on.

There was a pot-bellied man standing in front of the miniature TVs.

"Aren't they small!" she said.

"Yeah," he answered, never taking his eyes off Jim Palmer.

"Who makes them?" she asked.

"Emerson," he answered, still glued.

"*All* of them?" she asked, as though it was too much even to imagine that one itty-bitty little company could make all those adorable little TVs. She was giggling quite uncontrollably now.

"No, one's a Panasonic."

"Really!" She shifted her handbag, preparing to touch in a non-threatening way.

"Hon, over here," he yelled at a middle-aged woman loaded down with shopping bags who suddenly appeared. He walked toward her without a backward glance. (Single women should know that married women are using the electronics department as husband-sitters.)

While Cheryl was humiliating herself over a married man, Laura was creating a field of laughter near the Japanese tour group.

"Why are you shopping for appliances here instead of at home?" she asked one fellow, ready for a nice chat about tariffs.

"I don't speak English," he answered.

It was three twenty-five now. People had bought whole entertainment systems since we'd arrived. All we'd done was stand pigeon-toed in front of some young men who turned out to be college students.

It was at this moment that we were approached by a third woman. She wasn't wearing a badge, but she had Store Security written all over her.

"Excuse me," she said in a pointed manner. There was no field of laughter surrounding *her*. "May I help you? Is there something specific you want in this department?" She seemed prepared to touch us in as threatening a manner as necessary.

We took the hint. We left. No phone numbers. No dates. Lucky to still have our Field's charge cards.

A letter from a reader spurred our next field trip. It was from Patty who works in a laundromat. She suggested that they were vastly underrated as places to meet people. She went on and on, making us believe that the only difference between our local Laundry World and a Club Med is the suds.

"Men come in, see that you're young and female, and start with their questions," wrote Patty. You know, the usual: Should I use bleach with this? Can I wash my jeans with my underwear? What happens if I put my shower curtain in the dryer?

"They're so grateful if you help them. I've had men offer to help me fold sheets while they're waiting for their load to dry. One younger guy started folding my laundry for me while we were talking. I did object to the underclothes. I said, 'I'll take care of those myself.' "

Patty told us that we could learn a lot about a man by watching his laundry behavior. Does he hang up his clothes or crush them into his bag? If he's a crusher, you could have a slob on your hands—or worse: someone who's got a little woman at home, standing ready at the ironing board. Just the fact that he's even there tells you something: here's a man who values clean clothes. When you meet a man in a bar, what do you know about him? That he likes to drink?

So, based on Patty's experiences around the Maytags, we set off to see if we could spend a couple of hours at Laundry World and come home with more than bleach stains. We had Patty's advice ringing in our ears: "Start by casually talking to men. Start with, 'Oh, your wife stuck you with the laundry?' Then you'll find out if they're married. Most of the time they say, 'She's working.' But a lot of them are single. Ask men for change or if the soap machine is working. Sometimes that will start the ball rolling. All you have to do is be friendly and ask those key questions."

Well, we're reporters. Questions are our lives. We knew we could handle this assignment. We entered our first soap palace. It was ablaze with fluorescent lights. (Who can look good under these conditions?) We marched past the heavy-duty Big Boys and Speed Queens, and honed right in on two men folding sheets.

Ask questions, Patty had advised us. So we asked.

"Are you guys single?"

They were shocked. It seems that even today, men are not used to being approached this directly, at least not in laundromats. Yes, they were single, they finally admitted. No, they had never met women in laundromats. One, though, a twenty-three-year-old banker, said he had a friend who had: a woman approached the friend and asked for help. Her coins were jammed. We laughed knowingly. The sucker had fallen for what is possibly the oldest line in the steamy world of softeners and rinse cycles.

Moving on. (We were learning that laundromats are a lot like bars. If it's not clicking, keep going.) The next place we chose attracted a family crowd. One couple had brought dinner. In the corner, an impromptu bazaar was set up, with dolls and earrings for sale. But one young woman, a clinical psychologist in short shorts and a teeny T-shirt, was sorting whites from darks all alone. We asked her if she'd ever gotten lucky at the laundry. She said she had once met someone there, but "lucky" wasn't exactly the word she'd use.

"He was the biggest weirdo," she said. "He had on a black leather jacket and sweat pants." (We don't fault him for the outfit. It's possible all his other clothes were in the dryer.) "He said, 'I'll help you fold yours if you help me fold mine.'" Not only did she help him fold his clothes, she also helped him carry them out to his car. That was where he jumped her.

At this point, a twenty-five-year-old IBM saleswoman at the machine next to the psychologist's jumped into the conversation.

"I hate laundromats," she says. "I was robbed in one." Then, sitting on the washer, she went back to her reading. And we went home. A little older, a little cleaner.

The zoo was our own idea. Somehow we had this idea that it was just one big happy hunting ground for single, single-minded women who had targeted divorced fathers as their prey. While casually tossing peanuts to the elephants or strolling by the lions, their eyes would catch. Chemistry would bubble. And just like that, second families would be born. At least that's how we figured it worked.

So, we set out for the Lincoln Park Zoo in Chicago on a Sunday afternoon. Within fifteen seconds we found Gary. He was thirty-six, "sort of" divorced, and looked like Gary Fencik. He was a salesman and he had two adorable children that any woman would love to stepmother. He assured us he came to the zoo often and wouldn't mind at all if he met a woman there.

Gary made us cocky. If we had met him just like that, whom would we meet if we gave it a little time? We met Chris. He was twenty-eight, a construction worker, and he had a son, Chris Jr., age two. Chris, in jeans, with a bandanna in one back pocket, a thick chain in the other, and several holes in his left ear, was carrying a large brown bag that contained a diaper, a rag, and a change of overalls.

Chris had been divorced for a year and he said he didn't usually approach women when he was with Junior, but they came up to him all the time. Once he had a brief fling with a woman he met while he and his son were in line at a currency exchange. It was a conversation about "the terrible twos" that kicked it off.

"The women come up and look at him and say, 'He's so cute' or something," Chris said. "Eventually they'll get around to, 'Where's his mother?' "

Gary. Chris. At this point we felt the zoo was literally crawling with eligible men. Then we learned a couple of hard lessons. We'll pass them on.

Don't linger near the lavatories looking for guys. The men with the kids lolling beside the entrances may look like single fathers, but they turn into husbands the second their wives come strolling out of the ladies' room.

The food concessions are also the wrong places to look. You'll see lots of men standing in line all by themselves, or with a toddler in hand, but somewhere nearby is a hungry female, waiting for her man and her popcorn.

A further warning. Follow the man you've spotted for several minutes before you approach him with a casual, "Hi, do you know where the monkey house is?" Husbands and wives tend to separate by about five yards the second they hit the zoo. The father picks up their kid on his shoulders and the wife follows behind with an empty stroller. Watch for that nearby telltale stroller before you embarrass yourself. We learned this the hard way several times in one afternoon.

A field trip to a singles bar was aborted. We asked a bar-hopping friend what the secret was to meeting men in bars and she said it was "eye contact." She explained that when someone interesting looks at you, "stare back at him. Smile provocatively. Lift your glass in his direction. Wink suggestively. Pat the seat next to you. Mouth 'Hi.' Pantomime 'I think you're cute.' Anything. But above all never lower your eyes. Whatever you do, maintain eye contact!"

This turned out to be impossible. The minute that anyone even looked in our direction, we looked away. We looked over their heads; we looked at the person sitting next to them; we looked at their ties. We *tried* to look them in the eye. We just couldn't do it. We finally chalked it up to years of urban living, of keeping our eyes straight ahead on elevators and on buses, of decades of our mothers telling us not to talk to strangers. We've lost some natural instinct. So we stay out of bars.

We planned one more field trip. This one was to the Auto Show. This one we figured was a natural. What better place to find thousands of happy men? Some of them had to be single. We would find them.

They'd be in such a good mood with all that horsepower around. They'd be sure to think that some of that wonderful new leather smell was coming from us. They'd be on a natural turbo high. How could we miss?

Easy. We missed the turnoff for the show. The expressway was bumper-to-dented-bumper with cars all heading there. We couldn't get over to the off-ramp. We went right by it. We took it as a sign from God.

So, we decided to buy some Häagen-Dazs chocolate chocolate chip and rent *Gone With the Wind* instead.

That was our last field trip.

13

Men on Women/ Women on Men: What They Really Say About Each Other

What do men *really* say about women? Through the letters and calls we receive, we get to eavesdrop on them when they're baring their souls. Listen to what they *really* say. . . .

• I went out with a woman and it didn't hit me how young she really was until I mentioned Woodward and Bernstein. She thought I was talking about a law firm.

• You wouldn't believe all the women who ask me to do "little chores" around the house. These have included—believe it or not—rebuilding an entire foundation, clearing out seven acres of brush, and replacing a heating system.

• I introduced my daughter to a woman I was dating and my daughter started crying. I took her aside and asked her what was wrong. She said, "Oh, Daddy, can't you do any better?"

• I've been married, divorced, lived with a woman, and lived alone. And whatever I'm doing, eventually something else looks better.

• Dating around is like a series of job interviews.

• I'm forty-seven and I asked out this woman who's twenty-eight, twenty-nine years old. She said, "Don't you think I'm a little young for you?" I said, "No, but obviously I'm a little old for you."

• I paid close to $1,000 to join a video dating service and then I wasn't "selected" by anyone who saw my tape. It's a new twist: you get to pay a lot of money to be rejected.

• I'm tired of women with a dynamite personality. I'd settle for someone with a little heart and warmth.

• Women who want to get married remind me of Harvard graduates. They find a way of announcing it in the first ten minutes of a conversation.

• First she told me she wanted someone to take charge. Then she told me I was a little dictator.

• I can't stand women who read too many women's magazines. At the end of a date you know they're rushing home to fill out one of those questionnaires and you just know you're going to flunk.

• Women love getting flowers. They especially love getting them at work so everyone can see them get them.

• I was out of town, looking through all these little shops, and I thought, "I wish I had a girlfriend to buy something for."

• I get this sense of déjà vu when I'm going through a spurt of heavy-duty dating. I hear myself telling the same stories, making the same key points, sharing the same truths. I never remember whom I told what. I start prefacing every story with, "Did I tell you about the time I . . . ?"

• I've been putting personal ads in the newspaper to meet women and I've been averaging ten to seventy letters each time. The last time I added that I wanted somebody religious. I didn't get a single response.

• I could tell she had absolutely no interest in me until she asked me what time it was and I pulled back my sleeve to look at my Rolex.

• I asked a woman out on a date and she said, "Yes." When I called to let her know what time I would pick her up, she backed out saying she wasn't ready for a relationship. What relationship? It was a date.

• A lot of women have this problem that if they're not feeling loved every minute, they don't feel loved at all.

• I'm so sick of spending first dates hearing everything that's wrong with the last five guys a woman's gone out with.

• She pulled a "Starsky and Hutch" on me. The car was still moving and she jumped out.

• If you date women under twenty-three, you're okay. After that, it's a rare woman who just wants to have fun.

• The nice guys like me have to pay for the sins of the creeps.

• Women think all guys are interested in is sex. True!

• In a personal ad, "I'm a professional female" means "I'm a receptionist in either a doctor's or a lawyer's office."

• There are a lot of angry women out there.

• I recently asked my minister, "Where can I find a nice girl?" He said, "Good question."

• I've discovered a sure-fire way to avoid pain in relationships: overlap them.

What do women *really* say about men? Once again, we've eavesdropped through our column. Here's what we heard. . . .

• Who am I to complain about the men around? Look who Liz Taylor's going out with: George Hamilton, Michael Jackson, Carl Bernstein, Malcolm Forbes. Things are obviously tough all over.

• There have been so many Saturday nights when I've looked across the restaurant table and thought, "I wish I were home watching 'Love Boat.' "

• I was going out with this doctor and he'd call me at work and leave a message that *Dr.* Bellows had called. I thought, "What is he trying to do? Impress the switchboard operator?"

• Why do women always buy books about men? Have you ever heard of a man buying a book called *How to Understand a Woman?*

• Every time I fall in love, I lose five pounds. And every time a relationship ends, I gain ten.

• I walk into a party, and while I'm taking off my coat, I'm looking around to see if my future husband is there.

• He can call me in the middle of the night, come over at 3 A.M., tell me he loves me and how empty his life would be without me. But if I call him on a rainy Sunday afternoon and say, "I'm lonely. What are you doing?" he says I'm pressuring him.

• All the men who told me I was too good for them were right.

• After seven months of an intense, serious relationship, we had a fight. In the heat of it, I told him never to call me again. He said, "Okay," and he hasn't.

• Men who call themselves "the kid" should be shot.

• I had a note in my mailbox that there were flowers for me in the receiving room. I debated with myself whether they were from my old boyfriend or my new boyfriend. I ripped open the card. They were a promotion from the florist.

• Not one of my girlfriends has a husband or a boyfriend who could buy her an outfit she'd consider wearing.

• This man and I were lovers. We traveled together, we were as intimate as two people can be. But when I put in my contact lenses, he always turned his back.

• A friend saved up a couple hundred dollars to take a graduate course she needed to get ahead in her career. Then someone said they knew a great guy to fix her up with in Washington, so she used the money to fly there instead.

• When I'm on a roll, I knock down five to seven guys a year, like bowling pins.

• I'm tired of riding in the backseat of my married friends' cars.

• A terrible thing happened to a friend of mine. She married a guy and he turned out to be an honest-to-God bigamist. He had six wives. But you gotta say one thing for the guy. At least he can make a commitment.

• Someone once told me that in the beginning of a relationship both parties tell each other exactly who they are. It's true. When a guy tells you he's a jerk, believe him.

• I started dating a dentist. Then I noticed that the little white light on the top of a taxi cab looks like a tooth.

• I was trying to twist the top off a Diet Pepsi and I couldn't budge it. It made me think it might be nice to have a man around.

• I know he's a creep but I don't want to throw out the old dirty dishwater until I've got the new dirty dishwater.

• I wish all the women who are out there looking for a wonderful, responsible man would leave my husband alone.

• I'm beginning to think you don't learn the most important thing about a person until the relationship is over. There's nothing that tells you as much about a person—who he really is, what kind of character he has—as the way he says good-bye. Or doesn't even bother to say it.

• If all I wanted was casual, meaningless sex, I would have stayed married.

• I have a phone machine, I carry a beeper, and I just got a telephone installed in my car. Now when a man tells me, "I couldn't reach you," I know he's lying.

• A friend who just got divorced asked me what the best part of dating was. I said, "It's when the date's over and I'm on one side of the door and he's on the other."

• I'm a Ph.D. with my own successful business, enjoy theater and opera. The dating service fixed me up with a truck driver and a school janitor.

• He asked me if I wanted to go up to his apartment to see his computer programs. They must be the "etchings" of the eighties.

• My friend gave the woman he was dating a gourmet food basket for Christmas. I said, "Why didn't you get her something more personal —like lingerie?" He said, "That's much too intimate." I said, "You think buying her a slip is more intimate than sleeping with her? Something's very wrong here."

• There should be a service where you can locate a guy's ex-wife or ex-girlfriends and get the lowdown. It would save a lot of time.

• It's been so long since I've had a date that when this guy asked me if I was seeing anyone, I thought he meant a therapist.

• The best way to get over a broken heart is to break someone else's.

• He spent $400 on a gun then yelled at me for spending $29 on a blouse.

• We all thought we were smarter than our parents when we got divorced. The truth of it is that however lousy their marriages are, at least they have each other. We may have outsmarted ourselves.

• My girlfriends and I have two male friends that we all share and invite when we have to go to parties where you need an escort.

• You know there's something wrong with you when it takes you six months to get over a relationship that only lasted three.

• I work in a florist shop. You wouldn't believe how many men come in to buy flowers for their wives or girlfriends and ask *me* to write a romantic card.

• I'm thirty-seven and I've been dating for five years, ever since my divorce. The men I go out with remind me of the reduced produce at the grocery store. There's something wrong with every one of them.

• There are two kinds of women: those who break a date with their girlfriends for a great guy and those who break a date with their girlfriends for any guy.

• I couldn't believe it. He took me to the airport and actually parked his car, walked me in, and waited until my flight took off.

• I was talking to him on the phone and he was calling me "babe." I heard his little daughter in the background say, "Dad, which babe is it?"

• No one ever told me that just because a man loves to sleep with you doesn't necessarily mean he loves you.

• A relationship is work. You find yourself accepting things from a man you wouldn't take from a three-year-old child.

• He said I was chunky so I went on a starvation diet and lost all this weight. Then he said my clothes were baggy.

• I've been single too long. The other night I made myself a steak and I ate it standing up, tearing into it like a cavewoman.

• Even the end of a lousy relationship hurts. I've grieved over guys I never really cared about. It's loneliness and having to start all over again.

• I left messages for him all over town. I was trying to find him so I could break up with him.

14

Kids and Relationships

Today, romance isn't always a nice, clean "he" and "she." It often includes "his" and "hers." Kids, that is, not bath towels or toothbrushes. Kids: glaring, protective, suspicious, as in "Is that your *hand* on *my* mother?" Or sweet, loyal, and loving, as in "Will you be our new dad?"

When you're single, especially the second time around, the chances are good that the he or she you're getting will come fully equipped. You'll be talking babysitters and car seats somewhere around the second date. You might find that meeting someone with a child brings with it an unexpected gift: you get two (or three or four) for the price of one. Or you may find out it's like buying a used car: you get somebody else's troubles. Maybe it's a combination.

Split Roles, Split Loyalties

Suzanne was thirty when she got divorced, right in the middle of her prime dating years. On the other hand, her daughter was seven, smack in the middle of the years *she* wanted mom to be hers and hers alone.

So Suzanne compromised. She dated. In fact, she dated up a storm. But she was always discreet. She kept the men in her life away from her daughter, Tracy. She didn't have her dates pick her up at home. She met them at restaurants or in her lobby. Or she would see them on those nights Tracy stayed over at her father's.

"It wasn't like I made a hard-and-fast rule, it just evolved," Suzanne says. "I didn't need to discuss my social life with her. I didn't need these men to be part of our cast of characters, names my daughter knew. I didn't want her to have to live with me through whether he called or didn't call. We talked about sex but not about *my* sex life. She didn't want to know any more than I wanted to tell, so it worked out fine."

The years went by and the arrangement was holding. But then something happened. Suzanne fell in love.

"Then, of course, Tracy did meet Steve, and he would bring me home from dates—and he would stay over. But it was always after Tracy went to bed, and he would leave an hour or so before she woke up in the morning."

Suzanne didn't have it in her head to marry Steve (at least not right away); nor did she have a domestic fantasy of her, Tracy, and Steve teaming up as a cozy threesome. She still wanted to keep that part of her life precious and separate. But she also wanted to see Steve more than the two nights her daughter stayed with her father.

So, of course, there was tension. Tracy was not used to sharing her mother. One Sunday Steve came over for dinner and Tracy had a fit because Suzanne made spaghetti sauce from scratch. When it was the two of them, she would just open a jar. Another time he came over to watch a movie, and Tracy squeezed right in next to them on the little loveseat in the living room. "The three of us were sitting closer than in coach on an airplane," Suzanne says.

Tracy also felt free to yell at her mother in front of Steve and at Steve in front of her mother. "He was very good about it," Suzanne says. "He knew this was a difficult time for her and he never took offense. There were times Tracy would talk back to me and he would get angry, but he never showed it to her."

Suzanne had divided loyalties.

"On the one hand is a man I love and so, of course, I'm trying to present myself in the best light. And on the other hand is a daughter who was so needy. I had given her this false sense that I was *only* a mother and not a woman who had a life of her own."

Steve was patient about the sleeping arrangements. He wasn't thrilled about waking up at 5 A.M. every day, but he knew Suzanne wasn't ready to let Tracy see her as a sexual creature. Fortunately, Tracy was a deep sleeper.

Not deep enough. One night Steve had a cough, and it cut right through Tracy's dreams. She woke up and called out, "What is it?" Suzanne told her to go back to sleep. She said it was a bad dream, then she said it was the TV. But by then Tracy was standing outside her bedroom door screaming, "He's in there," calling both her mother and Steve horrible names and crying.

"It was a scene only Tennessee Williams could have done justice to," Suzanne says. "Steve got up and left. Then Tracy and I had it out, her calling me names and me saying that I was entitled to my life and she'd better get used to it."

That's when Suzanne began thinking that maybe she had outwitted herself in those early years when she pretended she didn't have a life of her own, that she was a mother only. There was no big-happy-family resolution to this one. Tracy slowly began to like Steve. Very slowly. But she did.

And Suzanne says, "If I had to do it over again, I *guess* I would still do it the same. I just didn't want her involved in my relationships. On the other hand, there probably was a certain point where I should have prepared her, so she didn't have to confront my other life at three in the morning."

Bachelor Father

Life as a single father is filled with adjustments: for example, which washroom does Calvin take his seven-year-old daughter Jen to when she has to go in a restaurant?

They used the men's room for a while, when she was much, much younger, and now they have switched to the ladies'.

"For a while there was a lot of me standing in front of the washrooms shouting, 'I'm out here. If you need anything, I'm out here!' " Calvin says. Things are a little easier now, but each day brings with it something new to learn.

As a single custodial father, he has had to learn what many mothers seem to know by instinct: he watched how they put barrettes in their daughters' hair, how they dressed them and cuffed their socks. From the edges of women's gatherings at playgrounds he listened to their talk of doctors and day-care. But he was on his own when it came to juggling relationships and a live-in daughter. It's hard to be a spontaneous bachelor when your life revolves around birthday parties and bedtimes—and when you like it that way, which Calvin does.

Once he met a woman at a party. They were interested in each other and he asked her out for the next night. She did a double-take when he came on that strong, but, Calvin says, "I have to be more structured than most people. I know exactly when my free time is. My life can't be open-ended."

Every bachelor father eventually plays out his own version of the scene from Kramer vs. Kramer when Dustin Hoffman has a woman sleep over for the first time. In the movie, Hoffman's son and his girlfriend meet in the hallway in the middle of the night, both en route to the bathroom. The kid is wearing pajamas. The woman is not. Calvin's version is not as dramatic, but he knows that having the woman over had to have had some effect on his daughter. What effect he doesn't know.

"I thought, there must be so much going on inside her head. But we didn't talk about it. You don't say to a child her age, 'How do you feel about this?' She'll tell me how she feels when she wants to."

In the morning, the woman, trying to play Mom, fixed Jen's hair. Jen didn't like it and she got upset. Then the woman got upset. And there Calvin was, having to console both of them.

Because of Jen, Calvin has had to define his relationships a lot faster. "There are a lot of things I wouldn't have to answer in my own mind right away if it weren't for my daughter," he says. "She sees me with a woman and says, 'Are you going to marry her?' And I have to answer."

Since Calvin's not in any hurry to tie the knot again, the answers to Jen's questions have been pretty easy. Still, he knows that many a tough Q and A session lie ahead.

Bachelor Mother

The other morning at the breakfast table, Nancy's eight-year-old daughter started smacking her lips making kissing noises and said to her brother, "I saw Mommy smooching with Sal on the couch last night." Not to be outdone, her brother replied, "Well, I saw her smooching with him in the driveway."

Here Nancy, who is divorced and thirty-five, was thinking she had had a private evening with her date "only to find out that four little eyes had been watching me." And that's not all. Endlessly vigilant and quiet on their feet, her kids have caught her with boyfriends in every room of the house except—she says gratefully—the bedroom.

What's a single mother to do?

In Nancy's case it has meant not having a really serious relationship in the four years she has been single.

"I wonder if it's because I have children," she says. "Other people may be able to jump right in and I know other women who bring guys home to spend the night. I don't. Here I am trying to teach values of love and commitment to my son, who's going through adolescence. So how could I have someone over, even though I know that as a single person there's nothing at all wrong with it?"

Immediately after meeting her dates, Nancy's kids begin to grill them, using the special vocabulary known only to divorced children: "Do you have kids? Who do they live with? How often do you see them?" And, of course, they ask her endless questions, too, including, "Do you love him?"

"They instantly think that if you see someone a few times you're going to get married," she says. "Usually if you're single, you do what you want to do, and if it's over, it's over. But if you have kids there are questions: "Why is it over? Are you ever going to see him again?" If they liked him, it's a loss, and divorced kids have already had losses.

"It's so complicated," she adds. "You have so many different people interacting. You have not only the two of you. You've got your own children and the person. If he's got kids, you've got his kids and you. Then you've got his kids and your kids. Did you ever do genetic formulas in school? That's sort of how I look at it in terms of all the different ways they can interact. All the people have to fit or you don't have a chance."

Her solution, she says, is to wait for a truly special relationship before she makes anyone a real part of the household—and in the meantime to "just keep laughing."

"You can feel so angry and deprived that you can't enjoy your single life, or you can keep your sense of humor," she says. "After all, despite the fact that I'm thirty-five, a professional, was married for twelve years,

I'm playing the dating game. My son and I are going through adolescence together.

"And you know what? My kids will grow up with a much more realistic attitude on life than we did; so in that way it's better. They don't believe in fairy tales."

Who Comes First?

One minute Peggy, a twenty-year-old college student, was struggling with English literature assignments, the next minute she was struggling with her boyfriend's two-year-old daughter, trying to change her diapers in the locker room at the neighborhood pool.

Talk about culture shock.

"I was really scared," Peggy says. "I hadn't been with kids before and I was jumping right into it. I was scared that if it didn't work out with the kids, it would blow my relationship with my boyfriend. I was scared that our relationship depended on my competence as a mom."

Peggy was involved with a professor with two kids; by their second summer together, since she couldn't find another job, she became the children's full-time babysitter while her boyfriend, Phil, was teaching.

"I enjoyed being with them despite my inexperience," she says. "It was when Phil was there that the pressure started. I was always aware of him watching me, wondering if I'd make them a good mother or not and I seemed to need constant approval, reports on how I was doing."

She came to love the kids. People even said they looked just like her. The little boy called her "Mommy" a few times and Peggy fully believed that at some point when Phil's divorce came through she would in fact become their step-mommy, "which was scary and nice at the same time."

Expected issues—including the all-time favorite, "Do I have the right to punish them?"—never arose. Despite her youth Peggy was a natural part-time mom and most of the time she got along beautifully with the children. Still, it was hard to hear Phil say, "You do realize that the kids come first?"

"I understood that but I didn't want to be hearing it in a relationship," she says. "I wanted to start out with me first but we started out with me second. Even though I understood, it still hurt."

Peggy began to feel the strain. When Phil came home from work, talk was about the kids, not always something she wanted to discuss, especially after being with them all day. When she needed to get away and be by herself, she felt guilty. And she never had any time alone with Phil.

"It was hard for me to admit I didn't want to be with them as much as I was," she says. "I thought to say that would be shirking responsibility. But I wanted to be free. I loved the kids, and him, but I needed freedom. I was too young to be involved in a relationship like that."

After three years Peggy broke up with Phil. That meant, of course, breaking up with the children too.

"I was very sad. It occurred to me that I loved them as much or more than him. But for the kids I have only love, so I am left with a warmer feeling about them."

About a year ago Peggy, now twenty-five, found herself involved with another father.

"I never met his children," she says. "I kept putting it off because I knew that knowing them would ultimately hurt me. More recently I almost got involved with a third man who had a kid. We had two dates and then a fight. I didn't pursue it. Lately I've been dating men closer to my own age."

A Package Deal

In the beginning, Michelle was afraid that her new boyfriend would be scared off by the fact that she was a package deal: she came complete with a six-year-old daughter.

That's quite a package to handle.

The three of them went Christmas shopping once, just a few months into the relationship, a time when you're still trying so hard for the other person to see you in just the right warm, golden light.

Unfortunately, Sally, Michelle's daughter, wasn't cooperating. She was really cranky and Michelle felt like pleading with her, "Cut it out, you're going to blow it!" Not a compelling argument to lift most six-year-olds out of a grouchy spell.

The nice thing was that Dennis, the boyfriend, *liked* it. He loved the fact that Michelle had a daughter. He loved the fact that he was slowly getting to know a little girl. That she knew the sound of his car and ran to the door when she heard it. That they were becoming a threesome.

"I'm sure that a lot of men are sort of scared off by a woman having a child," Dennis says. "But for me it has been more rewarding than any other relationship I've ever had. It's brought me a kind of love I never had before.

"Sally and I are crazy about each other. And one of the big things I like about Michelle is seeing the strength she has had in raising her daughter, and seeing the love between the two of them. It's not easy to raise a daughter that wonderful."

Sally came along on their first date. It was a casual thing, a daytime excursion to the beach. "In some ways it was better that Sally was along," Dennis says, "because there was less pressure on us. I sensed Michelle relaxing as the day went on."

Last weekend Michelle told Dennis that he would be a good father. It was one of the best compliments he could ever get.

"She has been able to see this in me," he says. "It's something she wouldn't have been able to know if it was just me and her. We are more than a couple. I feel I've been so enriched."

The couple makes a point of being alone, of course. And there are hassles: finding babysitters, a little girl who wants to be the center of attention and the focus of the love. But these are all minor to Dennis.

"I really am crazy about Sally. I love her personality; she's smart and she's sharp. We share so much: we have a lot of silly little games, little inside jokes, that kind of thing. We're into thumb wrestling now and it's so neat to be at a restaurant or be standing in line and just reach out my hand and she knows how to respond—and loves it."

Sally knows that Dennis loves both her and her mom. But she remains ever vigilant. Lots of times when he comes to visit, he brings Sally little presents. And once in a while Sally tells her mother, "I think maybe he likes me more than you because he gives me more things." It's clear that she wants Dennis to keep loving her mother (and to keep bringing the presents, too). She made him a Valentine this year: "Be My Mother's Valentine," she wrote in crooked printing.

"She doesn't have anything to worry about," Dennis says.

Kids in relationships: They mean commotion, crises, laughter, embarrassments—and lots and lots of extra love. There are so many second families these days, they may have to change the marriage ceremony to "I do" *and* "We do too."

15

Trouble in Paradise

(What really happens on romantic vacations, or never believe everything you read in travel brochures.)

There comes that point in every relationship—usually it comes pretty early, while she still thinks the beer foam in his mustache is sexy and he still thinks her morning-after raccoon eyes are cute—when the happy couple decides to plan a trip. And not just any trip. A really romantic vacation. They start looking at brochures and reading the travel section of the Sunday paper. They may decide to go to the mountains or the beach, to drive to Cape Cod or sail to the Caribbean—it doesn't matter. All that matters is they'll be together.

A Happy Day in London Town

While Princess Di was marrying her Prince, Ellen was playing house with her very own Brit.

She was thirty-five, a fashion buyer from New York, in Paris for the summer collections. On a whim she decided to fly over to London to see Mervin, a British journalist with whom she had once had a very hot but very brief fling.

They had met a year earlier when he was in New York reporting on British fashions for his newspaper. They had shared a couple of heady days: lasagna in Little Italy, pastrami at the Carnegie Deli, eggs Benedict at the Plaza. And when they said a poignant good-bye as he boarded British Airways, they both thought, "Let it go."

"I figured, 'Why pursue anything that has so little chance of leading anywhere?' " says Ellen, a sensible woman. "Neither of us were jet-setters. Neither of us were able to just pick up and fly across the Atlantic for a weekend. We had had a great couple of days and I decided the best thing to do was just file it away in my memory and get on with my life."

But fate stepped in. The head buyer got sick and Ellen was assigned to cover the Paris fashion shows. And while New York to London is a long and expensive flight, Paris to London is just a $99 hop.

The whole time Ellen was watching the models slink up the runway at Chanel and Dior, she was debating with herself: "Should I call Mervin or shouldn't I?"

On the one hand, she loved his wacky sense of humor and the sheer foreignness of him. He would tap the side of his nose to mean, "Watch this." She never knew if this was a British custom or just Mervin. He was

---

completely spontaneous and would wake her up in the middle of the night because he was feeling "a little peckish"—"It means hungry, not horny," says Ellen—and they'd head over to an all-night deli and feast on great big slabs of watermelon. And then, of course, there was that wonderful British accent.

But on the other hand, she hadn't talked to him in a year. Maybe he'd gotten married. Maybe he didn't want to see her. Maybe it was better not to mess around with memories.

But the French papers were full of Di and Charlie and the beautiful wedding that was going to take place in a few days and it was all so romantic that Ellen finally just picked up the phone and said, "Remember me?"

"He sounded glad to hear from me," says Ellen. "He said to fly over Saturday morning and take a taxi from the airport and let myself into 'the flat.' He had to work half a day. He'd leave the key under the doormat."

So Ellen did. Only to find a totally empty apartment. No sofa, no chairs, no tables. No bed. Just a lot of cartons piled up everywhere, and a very narrow cot. Ellen stood there for a few minutes and considered returning to the airport and catching a flight home.

"I would have done it, if the phone hadn't rung," says Ellen.

It was easy to find the phone. It was sitting on the floor in the middle of the empty living room. It was Mervin. He was glad she'd found "the flat." Just hang on, he'd be there in fifteen minutes. So Ellen sat down on her suitcase and waited. About half an hour later, Mervin breezed in. He was delighted to see her, they'd have a wonderful visit, but first they had to do something about "the flat." Specifically about the bed. They had to buy one.

Mervin lived just off Oxford Street, one of London's main shopping areas, so as they walked over to Selfridges department store he explained that he had just moved into his "flat," after years of living in a furnished one. He hadn't had time to buy anything.

They took the escalator right up to beds. Mervin picked out a very nice mattress and box spring and frame and asked the salesman how soon he could have it delivered. "In ten days, sir," said the salesman. Mervin turned to Ellen, tapped his nose, and took the salesman aside.

"I'd like to have a little word with you," he said.

"They were gone about fifteen minutes," says Ellen. "I thought I'd never see either one of them again. Then Mervin came back, rubbing his hands and saying, 'Right, then. That's all taken care of. Now, while I pick out the sheets and what-have-you, why don't you show these very nice gentlemen where the flat is.' I looked past him and there were all these men carrying the mattress and box spring."

And that's how Ellen came to lead a small army through the heart of London in the middle of a beautiful summer afternoon.

"I do remember thinking to myself, whatever I do in my life, nothing will ever be weirder than this."

The next four days were a blur of restaurants, sightseeing, and love. Tandoori chicken in Mervin's favorite Indian restaurant, hot and sour soup in a little dive in Soho, kippers at the Savory Hotel. Mervin took Ellen to every off-beat spot in London. They drove into the countryside and spent a night in a little inn outside of Cambridge. It was magic. And then it was time to go.

"It was sadder than the first time because we knew each other better and had more memories, but nothing had really changed. We said good-bye and we both went on with our lives. But, you know, it's funny, every time I see a picture of Princess Di, I smile."

Hanky-panky at the Taxpayers' Expense

Steffi and Doug, a state legislator, planned a romantic interlude at the taxpayers' expense. He would combine business with pleasure. Love on an expense account. He had to be in Boston for a five-day conference and he wanted Steffi to join him. It would be fabulous. Five days in Boston and then another week driving through Cape Cod, up to Maine, and over to Canada. They talked about it every day for three months. It was going to be a trip to remember. And it was.

They knew each other through work. She was a secretary; Doug was a friend of her boss. They had known each other casually for three years before they began to date and she knew all about the women in his life. Particularly Wanda.

Doug and Wanda had had a love-hate relationship that had dragged on for years. A few months after it was finally over, Doug began pursuing Steffi with gusto. She says he put on "a full court press." She played it cool for a month, but then she fell, and she fell hard.

Doug had to be in San Francisco, at *another* conference, just before the Boston trip. He called Steffi three times while he was gone to tell her how much he missed her and what a great time they'd soon be having. He was going to fly directly from San Francisco to Boston. She was going to drive his car there and meet him. She decided to call him as she was setting out on her cross-country car trip. It was 3 A.M. in San Fran when she dialed his number. There was no answer in his hotel room.

"I shrugged it off, telling myself he must be partying," says Steffi. In her heart she knew he was not a party animal. In fact, there was no good place for him to be at three in the morning other than a hospital emergency ward.

They both arrived in Boston on Sunday and Steffi was ready to let the good times roll. Doug was not. Instead of sneaking away from his seminars so he could be alone with her, he filled his days with nonstop golf. He spent six and seven hours on the links. It was a lot of teeing off. Steffi was a little teed off herself. So she showed herself the sights. She walked around Harvard and the waterfront. One day she paid $6 for a scenic boat ride of the bay and was so depressed she blew another $25 on drinks during the three-hour cruise.

The nights were no better. Instead of exploring quaint little out-of-the-way places, Doug arranged for them to join huge groups of people for dinner. When they finally got back to their hotel room, he was either so drunk he passed out or else had to go right to sleep because he had an early golf date the next morning.

On the fourth day, Doug ordered a room service breakfast before going on to his golf game. When the waiter came with the food, Doug was in the shower, so Steffi fumbled around in his wallet, looking for a tip. A picture fell out. It was Doug and Wanda—remember her? the old girlfriend?—in San Francisco.

No words needed to be spoken. Steffi saw it and Doug knew she saw it. That night he tried to make up with her. He arranged for them to go for a private boat ride. While they were on the deck, having a drink, Steffi confronted him. He admitted he had seen Wanda (How could he deny it?), but he swore that they were not back together. He told Steffi he loved her and that he wanted her in his life. That was when she threw her drink in his face and demanded to be returned to shore. The next day she flew home. She's still planning to see Cape Cod, but with someone who means it when he says "I love you."

The Pre-honeymoon Honeymoon

Do you dream about the totally spontaneous, perfectly adorable lover who whisks you off your feet and flies you away to exotic places?

Maggy found him.

She met Joe through a video-dating service. They both promised they'd never mention *that* again. They were both in their thirties, both divorced, both veterans of many, many fizzled affairs. On their first date he told her he thought he could fall in love with her. She didn't say it, but she thought the same thing. The next day, her birthday, he came to her office with flowers and a beautiful poem he had written for her. That night he called.

"He said he had a great idea," says Maggy. "He would pick me up on Friday and we'd go away for the weekend, to either New York, Boston, or Toronto. It would be a surprise. I'd never done anything like that but it sounded wonderful."

Maggy said yes.

Joe called every night and they tried to get to know each other. It's one thing to go away with someone slightly unknown; it's another to fly off with a complete and total stranger. Someone you know nothing about. Is he a crab in the morning? Does he have a temper? Does he like to cha-cha? Maggy tried desperately to find out.

"We had the most wonderful conversations," she says. "I kept thinking, 'This is how it's supposed to be. Easy. Fun.' We were both scared. We kept saying, 'What if we hate each other?' But we knew we wouldn't hate each other. We decided the worst that could happen was that we wouldn't fall madly in love. So we'd be two friends in an exciting city. What's wrong with that?"

Friday morning arrived and Maggy was a "nervous wreck." Joe picked her up. They had champagne and orange juice at her apartment and then they set off for the airport. He still wouldn't tell her where they were going.

"We were so nervous we got to the airport an hour and a half early. It wasn't until we got to the gate that he told me we were going to Toronto. I'd never been there, so that was terrific. We sat near the front of the plane, and we were giggling and carrying on the whole flight. We were the entertainment for all the passengers. He was kissing me. I was kissing him. We must have looked like newlyweds. As we were landing, he was nuzzling me so much the stewardess gave him a bottle of champagne and said, 'Here, hold on to this.' "

They checked into their hotel and the bellhop just wouldn't shut up. He insisted on explaining the amenities of the hotel and the joys of Toronto, and all the while, the two of them were waiting to jump on each other. "He finally left and we wound up staying in bed all afternoon and all evening. We ordered room service for dinner."

They spent Saturday shopping. Joe bought gifts for Maggy, her daughter, and his son. They had lunch overlooking an ice skating pond.

"He looked into my eyes and told me he was falling in love with me. He said I was perfect. He wanted to know why I had been divorced so long. He couldn't believe I was still available."

Maggy told him a little about her romantic history. She admitted that she was very picky. "I'm tough on guys, I know it. One guy came to the door in white shoes and I could hardly speak to him."

That night, Maggy and Joe were getting dressed to go to a very expensive, very discreet restaurant. Joe came out of the bathroom in a beautifully tailored navy blue pinstripe suit, a perfectly pressed white shirt, a subdued maroon tie, and bright orange tennis shoes. The brightest orange Maggy had ever seen.

"He said, 'This is for the guy in the white shoes. I'm getting even for him.' I laughed and then I said, 'Enough already. Change your shoes.' But he refused. He said he was going to teach me how unimportant appearances really were. He was going to show me I could have a wonderful time with a guy in orange shoes. All night long he pranced around in those awful shoes. I never laughed so much in my life. Or had a better time."

They were supposed to leave Sunday, but Joe begged Maggy to stay one more day. He wanted to take her to Niagara Falls for their pre-honeymoon honeymoon. He bought her a ring, a $13 fake gold band, and they became engaged-to-be-engaged in front of the Falls.

"He put the ring on my finger and said he had never felt this way before. He said I was the woman he'd been waiting his whole life to meet and that he would always love me and cherish me. It was a beautiful moment."

The next morning they went sightseeing. Joe said he wanted to take "tourist pictures," so wherever they went, he took pictures of tourists. He told her they would fill up album after album of tourist pictures as they grew old together.

And then they flew home. They picked up Maggy's daughter and Joe formally asked her if he could have her mother's hand. She said she would be delighted.

But it wasn't to be. Joe was the romantic equivalent of a sprinter, and Maggy was looking for a long-distance runner. While she was eager for the relationship to become ordinary, he was looking for his next high with someone else. But Maggy has some wonderful memories. She also has the tackiest tin ashtray of Niagara Falls you ever saw.

Rocky Mountain High and Low

Dan and Sharon went in another direction to find a little magic. They were Colorado-bound, and for the first few days at least, the vacation was shaping up as a real Rocky Mountain high. There they were, driving up mountain roads, exploring restored gold mines. The food was good, the high-altitude air invigorating, the hotel a find. They were having such a good time they even thought about extending their trip for a few days to get in some skiing. But there was one nagging little problem during those first few wonderful days: Dan noticed that Sharon was spending an awful lot of time shoveling quarters into pay phones.

"I didn't think a lot about it," says Dan. "She said she had a friend in town she hadn't seen in a couple of years and she wanted to get in touch with him. I kept saying things like, 'Great! Why don't you meet him for lunch?' I'm an agreeable guy. On the third day, she finally contacted him. She said, 'We're having lunch, I'll see you later.' Again I said, 'Great!' I wanted to do a little shopping anyway. I thought we would get together later."

Later grew into much later. By nightfall of the day of the lunch date, Dan began to wonder. He had always been under the impression that even long lunches usually terminated by three o'clock. (This one eventually went a record thirty-six hours.) Dan broke up the time by periodically trekking down to the hotel switchboard to ask if any messages from the missing Sharon had come in.

Finally, a day and a half after she'd left, a remarkably unremorseful Sharon waltzed into the hotel room.

"We had this big discussion like, 'Where were you?' and she nonchalantly said, 'I had lunch with an old boyfriend of mine, we got along real well, and I think maybe I'm going to stick around.' I was going crazy. I remember slapping my head a lot. I was trying to understand, but I wasn't having a real good time of it. In fact, I was saying a lot of real bright things like, 'I don't understand!'

"In the midst of this argument, I was calling her 'unreasonable' a lot. She said no, taking off wasn't an unreasonable thing to do, but this was, and bang—she bopped a bottle right over my head."

But that wasn't the worst of it. Dan had charged everything on his credit card: hotel, meals, plane ticket. And for months after, the bills came in. "It was like getting a picture of your girlfriend with another guy every single month," he says.

Which is probably the best argument we've ever heard for paying cash.

Balmy Breezes and Tropical Diseases

Penny thought she was heading down to Margaritaville when she and her husband, Ryan, traveled South of the Border for their third wedding anniversary. She found them a three-day–two-night trip from Mexico City to Acapulco via a "first-class tour bus."

"First of all," says Penny, "the 'first-class' bus had no air conditioning and the bathroom was broken. The trip took about eight hours. Luckily we did make a few stops in between. Needless to say, the condition of the public restrooms was awful. My husband was no help. He kept complaining about the dirt and he doesn't speak Spanish."

But finally the eight hours were over, and Penny and Ryan arrived at their hotel. They showered and changed and decided to have a quiet, romantic dinner in the hotel's Italian restaurant. This was, after all, their anniversary. And the restaurant was enchanting. The candlelight cast its golden glow over their soon-to-be-suntanned faces. The wine mellowed their good mood and aroused their senses. Penny and Ryan looked deep into each other's eyes. They toasted their good fortune, they drank to their continuing love, and then Ryan stuck a fork into his squid and that was it for that romantic dinner.

"He ended up in the bathroom all night," says Penny.

The next morning they tried to get their romantic vacation back on the right track. They went down to the hotel coffee shop for breakfast before setting off for a day of fun 'n' sun. This time, Ryan took one sip of milk and got deathly ill. He lost what was left of his dinner in the hotel lobby while making a run for the bathroom. Penny asked the manager to contact the hotel doctor. By now Ryan had a fever and it was rising.

The doctor prescribed some medicine. But the hotel pharmacy was closed and Penny had to walk several blocks, through what had now become enemy territory, to fill the prescription. Ryan slowly returned to human form and was later able to sit quietly by the pool (in a chaise longue near the bathroom).

On the morning they left, they had a full ten minutes to stroll hand in hand along the beach, speaking softly no doubt of passion among the palm trees. And then it was time to get back on that "first-class tour bus."

"Halfway through the bus ride we were stopped by some soldiers who ordered all the men off the bus," recalls Penny. "I didn't know what to expect, but they had their guns pointed. My poor husband couldn't understand what the soldiers were saying. Luckily, all the men were finally ordered back on the bus and we continued our trip."

In spite of that disastrous vacation ("I got in about one hour of sun in those three days and no dancing," says Penny), the couple has gone on to celebrate their fourth anniversary and are expecting their first child next year. And now they spend most of their romantic vacations at home.

Fantasy Island

What happens when you try to return to Fantasy Island? Thomas Wolfe said, "You can't go home again." But can you return to paradise? Gwen gave it her best shot.

She's a publicist for a major, major corporation. It's the kind of job that comes with lots of freebies. One was a business junket to a tiny island off the Australian coast. She and her American colleagues were in the Land Down Under to be wined and dined and provided with the best the exotic little island had to offer. Including Ian.

He was the captain of the fishing boat chartered for the amusement of the Americans. He was tall and rugged with an accent rough enough to sharpen a machete. Macho, but tender, too. "He told me I was his beautiful, warm lady from the other side of the moon," sighs Gwen. You can tell from her sigh that she doesn't think it sounds corny.

By their third day together she knew she was in deep trouble. She's the kind of woman who likes to be in control and she was spinning out of it. But she didn't care. "It was one of those rare experiences where I felt I was as much in love—and at the same moment—as he was with me. How often does that happen?" she asks.

Gwen was supposed to leave the island after five days. She stayed on for an extra week, and when the time came to go, the final morning was more Barbara Cartland than Thomas Wolfe. She was on one boat heading toward the mainland; Ian was on another sailing out to sea.

"It was pouring and I was on the bow in a raincoat with my hair all flattened around my face, the wind whipping it. And we just looked at each other across the boats," she says.

Now, what real-life workaday fella can compete with the Australian captain of a fishing boat last seen in a raging rainstorm? None, obviously. When she got back to the States, Gwen couldn't get Ian out of her system. She had to know whether it was just an island romance or something more. Several months later she decided to return to paradise.

Their first day reunited was a little awkward. Gwen had forgotten that Ian had this little habit of drinking himself into a stupor. The second day was even more awkward. She was in his room, trying to wake him, when another woman walked in carrying a bag of groceries and looking very much at home.

"Are you Gwen?" she asked.

"Yes," Gwen answered. "Who are you?"

The two women became acquainted over the captain's inert body.

"Then I just left," says Gwen. "I had come two thousand miles to see this man again and I just left. I didn't have the confidence in myself, I didn't have the confidence in the relationship, and I guess I didn't have the confidence in him to tell her to get out. I should have fought for him but I didn't have the guts." Six years later, she still carries Ian's picture in her wallet.

Gwen thinks the moral to her story is: "Fight for your man." That's not it. The real moral is: They don't call them "fantasy" islands for nothing.

The Real Love Boat

Life is like one continuous episode of "The Love Boat" for Hollis, twenty-seven. Not that she has ever stayed home on a Saturday night to watch it. When she took a real cruise on an Italian liner—five islands and San Juan—she promptly fell in love with one of the ship's captains.

Mario was older, forty, from a small town in Italy. Married, of course. Unhappily, he swore. Unwilling to divorce his cheating wife because of their adorable three-year-old son, on whom he doted. Naturally. But he was charming, handsome, and romantic with an irresistible accent. He was the first older man Hollis had ever known and she went for him head over sandals. At the end of the cruise, he told her he'd catch up with her in San Juan.

So Hollis checked into her hotel in Puerto Rico and promptly went to a cabaret. And there, in some dim, exotic bar, she met a Cuban jeweler. He was charming, handsome, and romantic, with an irresistible accent, too. And single on top of it. Closer to her own age. And rich. His family owned a chain of jewelry stores.

"I fell madly in love with him and forgot all about the ship captain," recalls Hollis. "Then two days later, I came in from the beach and there was a message at the front desk that a man had been waiting for me all day in the lobby and that he'd be back in half an hour. I had a date that night with Orlando, the Cuban jeweler, and ten minutes before he was due, Mario, the captain, showed up. He said, 'You meant so much to me. Do you think this is just a game?' He had tears in his eyes. I said, 'Come on, you probably meet a woman on every cruise.' He said, 'Not that often.' Then he left and five minutes later Orlando picked me up."

Orlando took Hollis home to meet his family. She had dinner there four nights in a row. He asked her if she would learn Spanish, if she could be happy living in Puerto Rico, if she had any interest in the jewelry business. She answered yes to all of it. The day she had to leave was traumatic.

"Crying and everything," is how she describes it.

The night she got home Orlando called. And he called again each night for a month. "My mother thought for sure I was going to marry this guy."

Several months later, Orlando sent Hollis a plane ticket to Florida. His uncle had a condo there and they could play house.

"The first three days were nice. The fourth day we went to St. Thomas for the weekend with his cousin and his cousin's wife. When we got there, Orlando wouldn't talk to me. He would just speak Spanish to his cousins. I got angry and finally said, 'What's wrong? Why are you ignoring me?' But he wouldn't answer. We stayed two days, and when we got on the plane to go back to Florida, I said, 'You better tell me what's going on.' "

He told her. He was engaged to a woman in San Juan and she had found out about his Florida love nest. "I can't see you anymore," Orlando told Hollis. "It would jeopardize my engagement." He went on to explain a little bit about foreign affairs to her. Latin men are different from American men, he told her, and the simple fact of his engagement was no reason for her to ruin her vacation. He graciously told her to feel free to continue using his uncle's condo and that he'd take her to the airport when her week was up.

You can imagine how crushed Hollis was. As soon as she got to the condo, she changed into her bathing suit, oiled herself up, and went down to the pool. And that's where she met the Spanish pilot. He, too, was charming, handsome, and romantic with an irresistible accent. They spent the rest of Hollis's vacation together. And when it came to an end, *he* drove her to the airport. Tough for Orlando. Good for Hollis. Don't you love a girl who knows how to have a good time?

We all know there's such a thing as travel insurance. You can insure yourself against a sudden illness or a change of plans that causes you to cancel out of your trip. But maybe someday travel agents will be able to insure us against the vacations that we actually *do* take—and that never turn out as we'd expected.

16

Happy Endings

Let's face it, you have to kiss a lot of frogs before you stumble upon your prince or princess. But it does happen. One day you'll be kissing another bumpy old toad and you'll suddenly find yourself embracing the love of your life. It happened to Wendy and Ben, Tanya and Rob, Colette and Matthew, Sadie and Judd, Phyllis and Henry, Babe and Kevin, Marie and Warren . . . and it can happen to you.

When You Least Expect It

Wendy thought she had used up her chances at love. She was thirty-seven, a schoolteacher, and had been out there meeting men and going out pretty much nonstop for as long as she could remember. By the time you're her age, you've spent more of your life dating than driving. That's a lot of time spent wondering what to wear. Whether you'll like him, or he'll like you. A lot of falling in love and crawling out of it. A lot of highs followed by too many lows. A lot of joy, yes, but way too much pain. After two and a half decades of falling in and out of love, she was pretty much a love cynic and kind of burned out.

That was the pretty dismal place Wendy was at when she met Ben, forty-one, a divorced advertising exec. He didn't exactly have the rosiest view of love himself. *He* was in the process of a painful breakup and not terribly interested in diving in and, given his history, hitting rock bottom again. But he had a friend who insisted he just *had* to meet Wendy, so he agreed. Reluctantly. Like, "OK, I'll go because how miserable can any one date be?" He invited Wendy to a football game.

The day of the date grew closer and Ben, despite all his years of dating, began to panic at the thought of spending hours with a total stranger. So he called up Wendy the Saturday before the game and asked if she'd like to take a ride just to break the ice, and make the next day's date a little less traumatic.

"It was a gorgeous day," Wendy says. "We drove to the park and had a lot of fun. Then we went out for drinks. He brought me home at eight. He wanted to go to the movies, but I said I had a lot to do. I really did."

The next morning they went to brunch, attended the game, then Ben came back to Wendy's house and prepared a fabulous dinner: chicken, wild rice, wine, Bailey's Irish Creme. You get the picture.

The very next weekend after that, Ben asked Wendy if she wanted to go to the Super Bowl with him. "That's a silly question," she said. "Of course." This guy, the same one who a week ago was so reluctant to go on one harmless date, was coming on like gangbusters.

Let's pause for a moment though. Wendy is close to forty. There's scar tissue on her heart. She does not approach romance dewy-eyed and she's not easily swept away. "I'm very cautious and slow-moving," she says. "I always wonder what's going to go wrong. I keep looking for flaws and faults. But with Ben there didn't seem to be any. He was just really comfortable, like an old pair of slippers or a favorite pair of jeans."

To continue, and bring this happy tale to a neat little close: Ben began calling three times a day. Once he called twice from an airplane. They spent one weekend at his house in Michigan, the following one in San Francisco. Ben bought her all kinds of presents, silly little things, stuffed ducks and a candle, ornaments for her Christmas tree. He walked her into a jewelry store to have her finger measured. "It was that weekend that he started saying he was going to marry me," Wendy says. "I said, 'We'll see. It's a little premature.' But I thought he was probably right."

Last year they started looking for a house. And Wendy is so happy she sounds dazed. Even dewy-eyed. A condition she thought she left behind, say, fifteen, twenty years ago. "I'm not nervous," she says. "I trust it. I wanted it all and I got it."

There Are Flowers and There Are **Flowers**

There are flowers and then there are *flowers*. And the day that Tanya got a dozen long-stemmed red roses from Rob with a note saying, "Just because I love you," and from Russell a pathetic bunch of semi-wilted carnations bought off a street-corner Moonie, she also realized there is love and there is *love*.

Tanya is a twenty-nine-year-old paralegal. She was fixed up with Russell, a forty-year-old divorced lawyer with custody of his two kids.

"I liked him," she says. "He seemed intelligent. We went to different kinds of places and did unusual things, but his emotional highs and lows and his temper really started to eat at me. And he was very, very critical. He didn't like my hair, he didn't like my makeup, he didn't like my clothes. He would prey on my vulnerabilities and point out my faults to others. I tend to exaggerate when I tell stories. If I said, 'I was laughing so hard I was hysterical,' he would say, 'Hysterical? Don't you think you're exaggerating again?'

"It reminded me of the teenage girl in *Up the Down Staircase* who sent a love letter to her English teacher. He returned it with the grammar and the spelling corrected. You can imagine how foolish she felt. Well, that's how he made me feel."

This went on for nine months. Maybe Tanya didn't think she deserved any better. Maybe she didn't think there was any better. Maybe she didn't know and was afraid to find out. But the final straw came the night they went to a symphony with two other couples. Tanya got all dressed up in a snappy red-and-black pants outfit. "I really thought I looked sharp," she says. Russell obviously didn't agree. "He didn't say a word, he just sat in the car fuming. He was literally grinding his teeth."

They met the other couples at a Greek restaurant. When the waiter took his order Russell announced, "I hate Greek food." At the symphony he refused to leave his seat at intermission. When the concert was over, he took Tanya straight home. The next day she finally told him it was over. She needed to be loved and he didn't seem capable of it. And then she said a little prayer: "Please God, send someone into my life so I won't be tempted to go back with him."

Tanya had known Rob, thirty-one, also a lawyer, for several years at that point. They had always been friendly but they had never dated. Two days after Tanya's prayer, Rob happened to look out the bus window at the apartment building where Tanya lives. Something clicked in his mind. He decided to ask her out for lunch.

"I was so nervous about the date," she says. "I was so used to having to be the one to put out all the effort. But it turned out to be so easy."

They started to see each other and every date was as easy as the first. Tanya couldn't believe it. She started testing Rob. She asked him to pick her up at her mother's house in the suburbs, something Russell would never have done. She asked him to have dinner with her family. Fine. Russell wouldn't even go to her brother's wedding.

Then last January Russell called. He needed to see her. He would pick her up after work. He arrived bearing that bunch of semi-wilted carnations, the kind you get on street corners. He told Tanya he wanted to marry her. They could get on the Concorde the very next day and fly to Paris for their honeymoon.

"Too late," Tanya told him. By coincidence, that same day she received a dozen gorgeous long-stemmed roses from Rob with a note. It read, "Just because I love you."

Mr. Fiero and Ms. Plymouth

At twenty-five, Colette thought she had met the man of her dreams and when the relationship ended she made the usual dramatic vow: "I refuse to date again until next year."

After four months Colette's friend said she had someone for Colette to meet, someone new to the area whose name she didn't even know but whom she had heard about from yet another friend. Colette said no way, she wasn't interested, but the friend phoned again and said she had just heard an incredible coincidence: the new guy in town was moving into Colette's apartment complex. She still didn't know his name, but she told Colette, by this time a teensy bit interested in spite of herself, that he drove a red Fiero so Colette should watch for the car and check the guy out for herself.

One day the car suddenly appeared in the parking lot and Colette found herself becoming more and more intrigued. So intrigued that she decided to make a move.

"I decided that since I didn't know who he was, I'd leave a little note on his car," Colette says. Her friend thought this was crazy but Colette's feeling was, "If he doesn't think it's funny, he's not for me."

So one night she set her alarm for 2 A.M. (she didn't want to be caught in the act), rushed down to the parking lot of the complex, and stuck a note under the windshield wiper of the red Fiero. First, though, she put the note in a plastic Baggie. "There was a lot of dew at that hour," she says. "The Baggie was to protect the note."

The message read something like, "Dear Mr. Red Fiero. I hope this note brightens your day the way your car brightens the lot." Colette signed it Miss Gray TC-3, referring to her Plymouth.

A week passed. Matthew, Mr. Red Fiero, was flattered. But it took him a while to put his own little note in a Baggie and leave it under the windshield of the gray TC-3.

"Please excuse our rudeness," his note read. "But the car and I had a terrible week at work."

This note-leaving—always in Baggies to guard against moisture—continued for three weeks, at about one note per week. Matthew and Colette had still never met. Once, though, there had been a close call:

"One day I was driving into the complex from one way and he was coming in from the other," Colette says. "When I saw his car coming I was so nervous. I thought, this is going to be it. I wasn't ready to meet him yet, so I drove on past the apartment. I drove around the block and when I pulled in he was already gone. I'm glad he was because when I got out of my car, I tripped."

It got to the point where Colette wouldn't leave her apartment unless her hair was perfect and she had on nice clothes—that's how scared she was of a chance encounter with Mr. Red Fiero. Finally she decided she *had* to meet him.

There was still a minor problem though. She knew his car, she knew his entranceway, but she still didn't know his name. So she walked over to his part of the apartment complex and knocked on the first door, which was opened by a man who weighed about three hundred pounds.

Colette's heart stopped. But then it flashed through her mind that this man could not possibly fit in a Fiero. He told her that the man who *did* own the sports car was named Matthew, and pointed to his apartment.

"I knocked on the door and he answered and I couldn't believe my eyes," Colette says. Matthew was impressed too. Still, it took him a few weeks to ask her out. Later Matthew told Colette that he thought maybe she just liked him for his car. In the meantime, there were several more notes.

Now they're married. Sadly, they had to sell the Fiero. But they have held on to the Plymouth TC-3. And, of course, they have kept the notes.

Berries Brought Them Together

"My love is like a red, red strawberry."

Sadie and Judd are entitled to a little poetic license. It was strawberries that brought them together and strawberries that kept them there.

It started like this: Sadie was new to Chicago. She didn't know a soul other than the people she worked with. Occasionally she and one of her co-workers would stop at one of the neighborhood bars for a drink. Other than that, her social life was pretty much nil.

One day she was walking down the street when she spotted a gorgeous guy heading into the neighborhood grocery store. Sadie decided maybe she should do a little grocery shopping herself and she followed him in and caught up with him in the produce. He was with another girl, but that didn't stop her. She went up to him and made grocery store small talk: "You think this melon is ripe?" "Are the peaches any good?" They tasted some strawberries together, then they said good-bye.

A couple of weeks later Sadie ran into the same man in a local bar. He was with a woman—a different one this time—and Sadie was with some friends from work. They both smiled and said hello. During the next month they ran into each other at least once a week in the neighborhood until finally one night they introduced themselves: "Hi, I'm Sadie." "I'm Judd."

It got to the point where Sadie was walking down the street two and three times a day looking for him. "He was seemingly nice and absolutely beautiful," she says. "I wanted to meet him, but I wasn't sure how to go about it. And he was always with a woman."

After many frustrating, lonely walks, Sadie decided to take action. She placed an ad in the Lost and Found section of the newspaper that read: "Lost: One handsome man by the name of Judd whom I met at the grocery store taste-testing strawberries about a month ago. Would like to meet for further taste-testing. Please write . . ."

"After I placed the ad I felt humiliated. I thought, 'Oh my God, what is this man going to think of me?' " At the same time she was thinking that, she was extending the ad for an entire week to make sure he saw it.

Monday came and went. Nothing. Tuesday. Nothing. Wednesday. The phone rang. It was Judd. He said he was definitely up for a little taste-testing. He said he never had the nerve to ask her out because every time he bumped into her, she was always with men and he assumed she was seeing one of them. She said she was afraid he was dating all the women she saw him with.

To make a long story short, neither of them was dating anybody, so they started going out. First once or twice a week, then after about a month or so they progressed to four or five times a week, and after four months they moved in together. Once Sadie got over the shock of Judd's being five years younger and still in school, they got along fine. A year later they were married. They put the finishing touch on a beautiful wedding by stopping by the grocery store and buying a box of big, fat strawberries.

P.S. I "L" You

Some people leap at love; others inch their way in. Take tiny little baby steps. For Henry and Phyllis, it was a matter of creeping up the alphabet from the "L word" to the "M word."

It took a while because Henry was twenty-seven and he wasn't really looking for a steady girlfriend. He was already juggling a handful of women. And when he was involved with one, the grass always looked greener somewhere else. But he was attracted to Phyllis, she liked him too, and they began to date. First on weekdays because the other women in Henry's life took precedence on Saturday night, America's Date Night. And Phyllis was pretty busy too. But after several weeks of Tuesdays and Wednesdays they worked their way up to Friday and finally Saturday nights.

It was their first Sunday together that was the breakthrough, though. It was a rainy, snowy kind of day. They had spent the night together. Henry put some records on, made them breakfast, and brought in the newspapers.

"It was nothing extraordinary, but it was the first time a low flame started to burn," he says. "We were comfortable together without talking. I remember leaving the room to get something and coming back and seeing her curled up reading the paper and that felt so good. I thought, 'God, this is great.' "

It was at that point that Henry started to back his way into saying, "I love you." Or as he puts it, the "L word."

"First, you just try to use the word a lot," he says. "You say, 'I really love pizza.' Or, 'I love the Cubs.' Then you move it up a notch. You say, 'I love your skirt.' Then, 'I really love being with you.' You drop it kind of harmlessly in the middle of a sentence. Then, in my case, I finally said, 'Would it be okay if I fell in love with you?' "

Since Phyllis did not run screaming out of the room, Henry decided to work his way up the alphabet. What do you know: they have now reached the "M word."

"First we started talking about other people's marriages and then kids, all very abstractly," Henry says. "Then eventually, 'I'm embarrassed to say this, but I've actually thought about marrying you.' "

Surprise again! Phyllis had thought about marrying him too. And for once, Henry is not worried about the grass being greener elsewhere. "I'm rolling around in the green grass right now," he says.

Of course he has doubts. He knows too many unhappily married people not to. He worries because she postponed telling him her apartment has roaches. What *else* might she be hiding? He wonders how much longer they'll stay up all night talking about their relationship. That's what you do in the early stages of a romance, but what if later on there's nothing else to talk about? His parents don't do that; they just talk. He knows that he and Phyllis are still in the "You like okra!! I'll try it too!!" stage of their relationship and that can't last either. He looks forward to its getting ordinary. But for now it's extraordinary. And that's just great.

The Reunion

Is there any person alive who hasn't looked at the invitation to his high school reunion with a feeling of dread? Is there any *single* person who hasn't opened it with a mixture of dread and excitement? Who hasn't thought that maybe now—five, ten, twenty years later, all grown up and well preserved—they'd find love among the crepe paper?

Babe was no different than anyone else when it came to her fifth high school reunion. Part of her wanted to go; part of her would have rather volunteered to receive a root canal. Most of her memories of high school were lousy.

"There were two groups in my school," Babe says. "The jocks and the cheerleaders and all their friends, and then the Mexicans and the black kids. And the two groups hated each other."

During her freshman year Babe, who is half-Mexican, went steady with a baseball player and hung out with the rah-rah types. Her boyfriend wanted her to go to bed with him and when she wouldn't he broke up with her and spread rumors about her all over the school.

"None of his friends would talk to me anymore," Babe says. "They called me names and threw stuff at me. I became pretty much a loner. Nobody liked me much. After a while, I started getting friendly with some of the Mexican kids who were in the class behind me. I started getting active in minority events and dances and clubs. My friends and I would cruise and listen to the oldies. The other kids were having parties and listening to rock and roll."

Since graduation Babe has kept in touch with a couple of her high school pals, Teresa and Carlos. They decided they would go to the reunion together. "I didn't really want to go; what was the point?" she asks. "I barely talked to anyone in my class when I was there, but something told me I should go ahead and go. It's like the prom. Even if you have a lousy time, at least you can say you went." Babe decided to wear a long black dress. She has bright red hair. "I was pretty wild looking that night and so was Teresa," she says. "We definitely stood out."

Babe walked in and immediately noticed Kevin. "He was really handsome and different from everybody else. All the other guys were dressed like cowboys in bell bottoms, heavy boots, and plaid shirts. They all had beards and sideburns. This guy had real short hair, nicely combed, and he was wearing pleated pants and a sweater and saddle shoes. I had no recollection of him at all from high school. I thought he must be someone's date."

During the night Babe was on the lookout for Kevin. At one point their eyes met. At another point she saw him sitting in a corner all by himself. "I wish he would come over here," she said to Teresa. He did.

"He started talking to Carlos. Then he turned to me and said, 'Did you go to school here?' I said, 'Yeah, did you?' "

Well of course he did. In fact, after much comparison of classes and schedules they realized they had been in the same ceramics class. In fact, they had sat at the same table, directly across from each other. Kevin vaguely remembered Babe. He remembered she was kind of tough-looking. He had been friends with the football and baseball players and it was obvious Babe wasn't their kind of girl.

She is now. If they were in high school, you'd say they were going steady. When they first started going out, they talked a lot about high school. They don't need to anymore. They spend more time on the present—and the future.

If at First You Don't Succeed

If at first you don't succeed, hang in there. It took Warren about twenty-two years and three tries to get what he wanted. Sometimes it just takes a woman a long time to make up her mind.

Warren and Marie first met when she was fifteen. He was seventeen and her best friend's brother. "I liked him, he was always very nice to me whenever I went up to the house, but there was nothing romantic," Marie says.

This was back in the 1950s. Marie became a high school senior and Warren went into the Navy. His sister—Marie's best friend—suggested that Marie write to him: letters to cheer up a homesick sailor. So they started corresponding and when Warren came home on leave he would drop by her house, often bearing flowers.

"A lot of times when he came by, I was on my way out the door to go roller skating with my friends or to the movies," Marie says. "He would stay and talk with my father. I liked Warren, but I didn't love him.

"Once when I was in a play he sent me a dozen red roses on opening night and made it a point to be in the audience. I found out later that he almost missed his ship."

Roses aside, Marie just didn't love Warren. She was in love with someone else, a boy she met her senior year in high school. She married him, and when Warren came home from the Navy he got married too. Curtain down on Act I.

Warren and Marie lost touch, more or less, but Marie kept in contact with her best friend, so she kind of knew what Warren was up to. That's how she knew he was divorced when her own marriage broke up after ten years and four sons.

"I called him for some advice," she says. "Since I had liked him so much once, even though I wasn't in love with him, I called him. He recommended a good attorney and helped me get back on my feet emotionally too."

The two began dating. But like before, they never got that magic timing just right. They never seemed to be in love with each other at the same time. Marie felt her feelings grow, but she wondered if it was a rebound kind of thing. Warren wondered if Marie was getting too serious too soon, and besides, he couldn't handle someone with four sons; he already had two of his own. He encouraged her to date others and she took his advice. But his feelings were stronger than his logic and he asked her to marry him. Too late. She had really taken his advice and she was involved with someone else. So she said no. Curtain down on Act II.

Six years passed before they saw each other again. The week before Christmas 1975, he called her for a dinner date. They started to date again and very soon after that he proposed—for the second time, on this their third go-round.

In advance he told her, "I'm going to propose to you in a few weeks and I want you to really think it over long and hard. Because if you say no this time, it's over. I'm going to finally get out of your life."

Marie thought about it for a long time. Then she said . . . yes! All six of their sons were at their wedding; the youngest joined the Navy last

July and by now Marie and Warren have been married more than ten years. They have the house to themselves for the very first time.

Neither of them regrets the twenty-two years that just happened to interrupt their lives together.

"He's a different husband to me than he was to his first wife," Marie says. "And I'm a different wife to him. All these years we feel we were growing. We've matured; we know what we want in life. Things that are important at twenty aren't so important at forty."

End of play. Applause. Applause.

Let's hear it for all the happy endings that followed some pretty shaky beginnings. And here's to kissing those frogs and watching them turn into the love of your life. It does happen!

Conclusion

We hope you enjoyed our tales. Both the stories of woe and of Wow!

We hope you've recognized yourself once or twice as you read about the Die-hards who won't admit when love's over or the lucky folks who found love where they least expected it, like aisle three of the grocery store.

We hope you're pulling for the Nice Guy to find a woman who appreciates him. For the Telephone Answering Machine Junkie to unplug her machine. And for Mr. Gotta Keep Moving On to settle down.

We hope you learned a lesson from Ms. Picky-Picky-Picky who pick-picks herself right out of the market and from the Sucker who keeps falling for the wrong women.

We hope you've taken heart in the fact that you're not the only one who suffers from the Carton Complex and has boxes stacked in your living room. That you're not the only one caught in the Déjà Vu Dilemma who has fallen in and out of love too, too many times.

Maybe now you'll be more likely to consider a mixed romance—or pay attention when the chemistry's right.

And maybe you'll think twice before you say, "I'll call you," or when you hear, "I have no wife."

We hope you've learned that you're not the only one who had a lousy New Year's Eve, who needs a date to take to an old flame's wedding, and who's sometimes lonely and confused. It's all part of being single.

But as one woman recently wrote us, "The best part of being single is knowing that one day I'll meet and fall in love with a wonderful man. It's exciting wondering when and where I'll find him." We couldn't agree more.

Most of all, we wish you well in your own adventures of the heart. May most of your tales be happy ones.

All the best from *Tales from the Front.*